CASTAWAYS

Latin American Literature and Culture

General Editor
Roberto González Echevarría
Bass Professor of Hispanic and Comparative Literatures
Yale University

CASTAWAYS

THE NARRATIVE OF
ALVAR NÚÑEZ
CABEZA DE VACA

Edited by Enrique Pupo-Walker
Translated by
Frances M. López-Morillas

University of California Press
Berkeley · Los Angeles · London

This edition has been translated with the help of a grant from the Dirección General del Libro y Bibliotecas of the Spanish Ministry of Culture.

The publisher also gratefully acknowledges a grant from the Program for Cultural Cooperation between Spain's Ministry of Culture and United States universities.

University of California Press
Berkeley and Los Angeles, California

University of California Press, Ltd.
London, England

Library of Congress Cataloging-in-Publication Data
Núñez Cabeza de Vaca, Alvar, 16th cent.
    [Relación o naufragios de Alvar Núñez Cabeza de Vaca. English]
    Castaways : the narrative of Alvar Núñez Cabeza de Vaca /
edited by Enrique Pupo-Walker ; translated by Frances M. López-
Morillas.
      p. cm.
    Translation of: Relación o naufragios de Alvar Núñez Cabeza de Vaca.
    Includes bibliographical references.
    ISBN 0-520-07063-1 (pbk.)
    1. Núñez Cabeza de Vaca, Alvar, 16th cent. 2. America—Early
accounts to 1600. 3. America—Discovery and exploration—Spanish.
4. Indians of North America—Southwestern States. 5. Southwestern
States—Description and travel. 6. Explorers—America—Biography.
7. Explorers—Spain—Biography. I. Pupo-Walker, Enrique. II. Title.
E125.N9A3 1993
970.01'6'092—dc20
                                                  92–25645
                                                     CIP

Printed in the United States of America

08 07 06 05

12 11 10 9 8 7

The paper used in this publication meets the minimum requirements of ANSI / NISO Z39.48-1992 (R 1997) (*Permanence of Paper*). ∞

Contents

Illustrations

Editor's Foreword

This translation is based on my critical edition of Cabeza de Vaca's *Relación* (Madrid: Editorial Castalia, 1992). Its textual basis is the joint edition of the *Naufragios* and *Comentarios* printed in Valladolid in 1555 (see the bibliography). I chose this edition, and not the original edition of 1542, because that one was obviously produced without Cabeza de Vaca's supervision; no doubt for this reason, it is plagued with errors and has a rudimentary format. The corrections in the 1555 edition point to the intervention of Alvar Núñez, who was in Valladolid at the time. My edition lists the variants found in the different versions of this text during the course of the sixteenth century and also comments on the most important editions that appeared in the eighteenth, nineteenth, and twentieth centuries. As an aid to reading, I offer a more convenient division into paragraphs, though without altering the arrangement given the text in 1555.

In my critical edition I identify geographical landmarks and the flora and fauna of several North American regions, as well as the chief pre-Columbian cultures mentioned or described by Cabeza de Vaca. In my introductory study to that edition I offer several analyses of the text and its relation to the *Comentarios*.

Acknowledgments

I am extremely grateful to the Guggenheim Memorial Foundation, the American Philosophical Society, and the Research Council of Vanderbilt University, for the generous help extended to me when I began my investigation of the *Naufragios.* Their aid afforded me access to libraries and archives in Spain, the United States, and Great Britain. In large measure this edition has been made possible thanks to the patient and painstaking editorial labors of Mrs. Norma Antillón, technical secretary of the Center for Latin American and Iberian Studies at Vanderbilt University. I also gratefully acknowledge the valuable cartographical help of Marilyn L. Murphy and the learned anthropologist Ronald Spores, both professors at Vanderbilt University.

Introduction

Governor Pánfilo de Narváez's expedition that set out on "the seventeenth of June in the year fifteen hundred and twenty-seven" consisted of five ships, and crews totaling about six hundred men. After sailing from Sanlúcar de Barrameda the ships made a stop in the Canaries and went on for almost three months until, in mid-August, they reached Hispaniola. On this island they replenished their supplies and Narváez attempted without success to recruit additional crew members. From Hispaniola they went to Cuba, where they spent the winter of 1527–1528 but experienced setbacks (chs. I and II). In Santiago de Cuba and in the town of Trinidad they gradually acquired the provisions that the expedition needed to continue on its way. The costs, it may be remarked in passing, were borne by Narváez and the wealthy Spaniard Vasco Porcallo de Figueroa, who was then living in Cuba and who, years later, joined Hernando de Soto's expedition. During the months that the expedition spent in Cuba, a hurricane caused fifty deaths and considerable losses of animals and stores, as well as sinking two ships. Cabeza de Vaca stayed with some of the crews in the Bay of Jagua at the entrance of Cienfuegos, while Narváez stayed in the Bay of Santa Cruz (chs. I and II). As Núñez confirms, they at last set foot in Florida on 14 April 1528, in a coastal area near Tampa Bay, perhaps very near Boca Ciega.[1]

Following a dispute between Núñez and Narváez (ch. IV), a party of about three hundred men led by Narváez struck into the peninsula, briefly marching east and later north, on a route parallel to the Florida coast (see figure 1); these were regions abounding in swamps, poisonous snakes, and harsh and noxious vegetation. Narváez had left a hundred men with the ships, which in their turn were to sail along the coast and

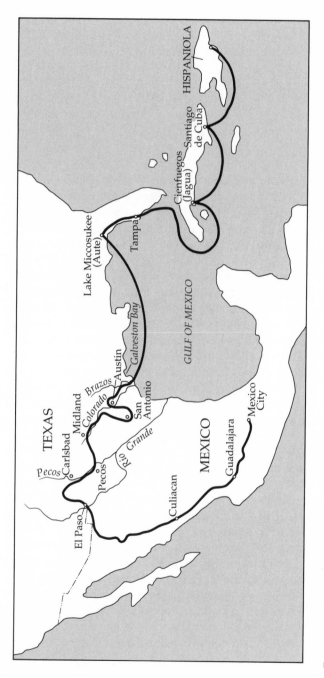

FIGURE 1. Approximate route of Cabeza de Vaca.

eventually make possible a meeting of the two groups. But these crews, guided by an inexperienced pilot, lost contact with the land party in a matter of days. In the end the ships returned to New Spain, giving up Narváez's group for lost. By the time this group reached the northernmost part of Florida, near the present-day city of Tallahassee, it had been diminished by exhaustion, illness, and the often savage battles with Indians (chs. V–IX). Very near a village occupied by Apalachee Indians, which they called Aute, the survivors of the expedition decided on the remarkable expedient of constructing boats in which to sail westward, following the coast that was their only guide; as they thought, the route would take them to already explored and conquered regions of New Spain. When the boats had been built (ch. IX), after terrible sacrifices, they embarked; but bad weather, hunger, thirst, and the strong currents of the Mississippi River (ch. X) caused the five boats of the expedition's survivors to drift helplessly. By the autumn of 1528, Núñez and some of his companions were left defenseless and destitute among groups of Karankawa Indians who lived on these coasts, now part of eastern Texas; perhaps they did not imagine that in this desolate region they would spend years of slavery and indescribable suffering. In the end, of the three hundred men who had landed in Florida four would survive: Andrés Dorantes, Alonso del Castillo Maldonado, the Moroccan slave Estebanico, and Núñez. The possibility exists that a Greek named Teodoro survived by joining tribes in that region. Other information, collected years later by Hernando de Soto's men, suggested that Teodoro was sacrificed by the Indians.

After long delays and detours Núñez and his companions journeyed toward the west, pausing at times with clans and tribes of Coahuiltecs, Jumanos, Opatas, and Pimas, among other Indians (see Appendix B). In their long pilgrimage Núñez and his companions had to survive under conditions of desperate need. Among those tribes they functioned more than once as medicine men or shamans. Always traveling westward, and later toward the south, Cabeza de Vaca and his companions finally met a group of Spanish soldiers (ch. XXXIII) who were laying siege to native communities in northern New

Spain. The long-desired encounter took place after eight years of wandering through deserts and inhospitable regions, amid severe climatological conditions, in nakedness and total lack of protection. But he tells us little about the joy and rejoicing that resulted from the meeting. Núñez and his companions at last reached the village of Culiacán on 1 April 1536. Castillo, Dorantes, and Estebanico stayed in New Spain. Estebanico was killed some time later, after joining the ill-planned expedition guided by Friar Marcos de Niza, when de Niza—encouraged by the viceroy, Antonio de Mendoza—was seeking the mythical Seven Cities of Cibola.

Núñez, with other ideas in mind, began his return journey to Spain from Veracruz on 10 April 1537 and disembarked in Lisbon on 9 August 1537. Cabeza de Vaca lived in Spain from his return until 2 December 1540. In that same year, after appearing before Charles V, Núñez signed on 18 March the agreements that would impel him toward another American adventure; but this time he went to the regions of Río de la Plata in command of three ships, and with the important ranks of *adelantado* and governor.[2]

Available information suggests that Cabeza de Vaca spent the twenty-eight months of his residence in Spain editing his already amplified *Relación* (also called the *Naufragios*); it was published in Zamora in 1542. He returned to these preoccupations years later in the prologue to the Valladolid edition of 1555; in that text (which appears in this edition) Cabeza de Vaca tells us, with studied humility, that since neither his

> advice nor [his] best efforts sufficed to win what we had gone to accomplish in Your Majesty's service, and because God permitted, for our sins, that of all the fleets that have gone to these lands, none found themselves in such great dangers or had such a miserable and disastrous end, no opportunity was afforded me to perform more service than this, which is to bring Your Majesty an account of what I learned and saw in ten years [1527–1537] during which I wandered lost and naked through many and very strange lands . . . that may in some wise be of service to Your Majesty.

At the time he was writing, Núñez must also have been concentrating his efforts on the arduous negotiations and preparations required by his expedition to Río de la Plata. Though the first edition of his text was published after he had gone to South America, we may imagine that the book had some acceptance among the limited circle of readers who acquired such a small edition. Today we know that the famous historians Gonzalo Fernández de Oviedo and Francisco López de Gómara read it. We may suppose that it reached the hands of other chroniclers and officials who wrote on such subjects and who traveled to the New World. Among them must have been Father Bartolomé de Las Casas, who was always well aware of everything pertaining to the indigenous populations of America.

In his detailed and enthusiastic biography of Núñez, Morris Bishop describes the jubilant return of the conquistador to Jerez de la Frontera and alludes to contemporary rumors about the fabulous things that Cabeza de Vaca had experienced.[3] Perhaps the most remarkable thing about his brief stay in Spain is that, when he returned to the Peninsula, Núñez showed an almost immediate interest in going back to the same jungles and deserts where he had suffered so many calamities. Scarcely had he landed in Lisbon than he must have learned that the Crown had appointed Hernando de Soto governor of Cuba and of all the region between Cape Fear (now part of North Carolina) and the river of Las Palmas, in New Spain. Quite simply, it was a territory about half the size of Europe. The appointment must have caused resentment in Núñez, and perhaps for that reason Hernando de Soto was unable to persuade him to accompany him on the adventure. Despite this, and much to Cabeza de Vaca's displeasure, two cousins of his—Baltasar Gallegos and Cristóbal de Espínola—joined de Soto, even though they were aware that Núñez was opposed to their going.[4] In only a few years, the Spain that Núñez had known in his early youth had become a society that was planning enormous imperial projects of conquest and colonization, projects involving powerful and adventure-hungry groups with overweening ambitions. Morris Bishop observes, when he reconstructs some features of this society, that Núñez must have felt alien to such a context, which in many ways seemed to him puzzling and excessively conflictive; it was a society in which so many men struggled—for good reasons or bad—to attain privileges, riches, and above all the eternally desired prerogatives of power.

We may assume that during this interval of residence in the Peninsula Núñez became connected with the large brotherhood of travelers, chroniclers, and officials who exchanged information about America as they made their complicated claims. Years later, in the carefully composed prologue to his *Comentarios* (edited by the scribe Pedro Hernández; see Appendix A), Núñez was to explain, with veiled rhetorical ambiguity, the mission of rescue that the Crown had entrusted to him in 1540, which would be carried out in the remote areas now occupied by Paraguay.

As we will see, the task entrusted to him gave Núñez governing authority over all the immense region between southern Peru and the areas now occupied by Argentina, Uruguay, and Paraguay. He explained the mission in these terms:

> Later, the Supreme Majesty having deigned to continue His marvelous favor to me, He caused the emperor, your grandfather, to send me in the twenty-first year of his reign with a fleet to Río Paraná (which Solís calls Río de la Plata), to help people and continue the discovery of Don Pedro de Mendoza (who they said was a native of Guadix). In which I experienced very great dangers and hardships, as Your Highness will very particularly see in these *Commentaries*.[5]

A large part of the abundant documentation on Spanish colonization in the region of Río de la Plata indicates that the project of territorial expansion had degenerated into opportunistic struggles that caused violent confrontations between natives and Spaniards. The scanty information possessed by the Crown, in the first half of the sixteenth century, suggested a need for drastic solutions. In view of his vast experience in the Indies and his knowledge of different American cultures, Núñez must have presented himself to the Crown as exactly the right person to carry out the task of correction and reparation. Thus, in the articles drawn up on 18 March 1540,[6]

Charles V granted to Cabeza de Vaca the governorship of Río de la Plata with the same prerogatives and territories that the Crown had previously accorded to Pedro de Mendoza. He also received the titles of *Adelantado*, Governor, Captain-General, and Officer of the Peace in those possessions, including the island of Santa Catalina, which today is part of Brazil. But even in those days of unaccustomed glory, Núñez encountered obstacles that anticipated the difficulties that were to pursue him, with cruel tenacity, to the end of his life. At the last moment, when all was ready for his departure, the Ayola family (with connections to the previous governor of Paraguay) attempted to lodge before the Council of the Indies an appeal blocking Núñez's appointment as governor; fortunately, direct intervention by the Crown sufficed to eliminate this obstacle. A royal warrant unhesitatingly ordered the House of Trade to assist Núñez in everything necessary for the voyage.[7] As rapidly as possible Cabeza de Vaca, then about forty-eight years of age, equipped three ships. His chief pilot was Antonio López, and the crews included a Flemish drummer and a number of Negro and Indian slaves, one of them a native of New Spain. Once again Cabeza de Vaca left his wife in Spain; apparently she always tolerated his prolonged absences.

In the late autumn of 1540 preparations for the long voyage were at last finished; but unforeseen delays occurred. It was not until the end of November that the ships began their descent of the Guadalquivir toward Sanlúcar. Scarcely had they emerged into the Atlantic than a spell of bad weather forced them to seek hasty refuge in Cádiz Bay, from which they succeeded in leaving for the Canaries on 2 December of that year. Once more Núñez was setting out for the New World from Andalusian soil, except that this time he was assuming greater responsibilities, and his position involved debts far beyond his economic means.[8]

The voyage took four months, including a short stopover in the Canaries. They landed on the island of Santa Catalina on 29 March 1541, and from there—after a long rest period— undertook the overland march to Asunción. Very soon Núñez learned of the murder of Juan de Ayola, the governor who had preceded him. These events convinced Cabeza de Vaca that he needed to attempt without delay to rescue the Spaniards who were thus left without official protection (*Comentarios*, ch. 1). After marching for more than five hundred miles, the contingent reached Asunción on 11 March 1542. In the course of that mountainous and difficult journey, the group led by Cabeza de Vaca was the first to see some spectacular landscapes, including the dramatic falls of the Iguaçú River. After presenting his credentials, Cabeza de Vaca tried to correct abuses that had been committed against the Indians and attempted to restore order among the Spaniards, obliging them among other measures to pay the taxes required by the Crown. Measures of this kind ran counter to the economic interests of a remote and quarrelsome colony and immediately caused disaffection and aggressive opposition on the part of many residents. The opposition was led by Domingo Martínez de Irala, who had been serving as interim governor. But the lengthy and interesting reports of Ulrico Schmidel, a German, as well as those of Ruy Díaz de Guzmán, suggest that Cabeza de Vaca lacked political acumen as well as the ability to carry out administrative and planning duties. According to Schmidel, his inept attempts at exploration gradually led him to repeated confrontations with Indians and Spaniards alike. Our information about these matters suggests insistently that Núñez placed more trust in individual action than in joint and institutionalized activity.[9]

Like so many others, Núñez was seduced by the fabulous promises offered by legends about priceless treasures; he organized a well-equipped expedition to discover those places of prodigious riches. But the sacrifices involved in a journey through trackless jungles caused resentment and illness, and Núñez at last decided to return to Asunción. There, weakened by long bouts of fever, Cabeza de Vaca began to lose control of his recently acquired governorship. His illness provided the vacuum of authority his enemies needed; in particular, Martínez de Irala and his supporters used it to foment a rebellion against Cabeza de Vaca's inconsistent leadership. Though a number of colonists fought the rebels' actions, on 25 April 1544

Martínez de Irala and his supporters took the governor prisoner. Perhaps to mute the protests among the Indians and Cabeza de Vaca's junior officials, Martínez de Irala decided to send the governor to Spain in a caravel that was returning to the Peninsula. With various accusations leveled against him, Cabeza de Vaca was held prisoner along with his scribe Pedro Hernández and others, placed in irons, and confined to a small and dark space on the ship. But apparently their confinement on board was short.

Apart from the inconvenience of these restrictions, the return trip to Spain added another paradoxical incident to Cabeza de Vaca's ill-starred life. Enrique de Gandía tells us that during the crossing the caravel in which Cabeza de Vaca was traveling encountered a fierce storm off the coast of Brazil; some of the officers on board, among them Alonso Cabrera and García Venegas, interpreted the bad weather as divine retaliation for the injustices committed against Núñez, who was after all the legitimate representative of the Crown. De Gandía states that the governor and his companions were set free and that the accusations against him were denied. Thanks to this fortunate occurrence Núñez was released, and the storm immediately began to abate. Though these events—influenced by legend, as I suspect—seemed favorable, we shall see that Cabeza de Vaca's misfortunes began again when he landed in Spain about 15 August 1545.

Cabeza de Vaca visited Seville and Jerez and in the same year presented before the Council of the Indies documents that attempted to refute many of his enemies' allegations. As was to be expected, the pardon issued on board ship was not recognized in Castile.[10] Núñez soon had to appear before the always unpredictable council, on 20 January 1546, to hear the numerous accusations from those who had usurped his command. He was accused, among other things, of robberies in the Canaries and Cabo Verde on his way to South America. The documents alleged that Núñez had not allowed his crew to trade with the Indians and that he had abandoned thirteen of his men on the way to Asunción. Documents in the possession of Marcelo Villalobos, the prosecutor, also described a long series of abuses that Núñez had supposedly committed against both Spaniards and natives. Still worse, he was accused of substituting his own coat of arms for the symbols of the Crown and of not allowing the other officers in his suite to communicate with peninsular authorities.[11] As if to emphasize the difficulties Cabeza de Vaca now faced, his economic situation grew difficult because of the debts that he had contracted in order to equip his expedition. A Spaniard who had met him in Asunción declared that the governor "owned not a real's worth in those realms." Cabeza de Vaca himself confessed in February 1546 that "he was poor and lost and bankrupt, he and his relatives alike."[12]

Early in 1546 when the suits against Núñez began, he was not permitted to use witnesses living in Spain. This frivolous restriction drew the noose still tighter and hints at the negative bias of the tribunals that were to judge him. The appointment of Villalobos as the prosecutor responsible for the suits against Núñez appeared to be a fortunate coincidence, for Villalobos, like Núñez, was a native of Jerez. But in the end this same prosecutor demanded large indemnities from Cabeza de Vaca, thus allowing his accusers to appear as the injured parties. Villalobos also demanded a fine of 100,000 ducats, which Núñez had to pay to the Crown. In view of this and other petitions, in March 1546 the Council of the Indies ordered the arrest and imprisonment of Cabeza de Vaca in Madrid. Very shortly later, in April of that same year, he was granted provisional freedom and allowed to live in lodgings in Madrid. In a more generous vein, the council granted Núñez three years to prepare his defense, directed by his lawyer Alonso de San Juan. But the defense and litigation lasted more than five years.

Gonzalo Fernández de Oviedo—who around 1547 met Núñez in Madrid, Seville, or Valladolid—tells us that he was "impoverished and prematurely aged."[13] It is almost certain that Fernández de Oviedo interviewed him to obtain additional information that he needed for his unfinished *Historia general y natural de las Indias*. But meanwhile the process of accusations and claims that Núñez had to face was becoming increasingly broader and more complicated. The documents necessary to reach a final verdict continued to accumulate, even into 1547. Examination of the documents suggests an increasing disinclination toward Cabeza de Vaca on the part of the courts. Finally, on 18 March 1551, in Valladolid, the Council of the Indies announced its sentence.

Cabeza de Vaca was stripped in perpetuity of the important titles he had been granted in 1540. He was also barred on pain of death from returning to the Indies and was condemned to exile and forced labor in Africa (Algiers). Moreover, persons living in Asunción who had claims against him as injured parties could now demand heavy financial compensation from him. Cabeza de Vaca immediately appealed this decision and abjectly begged the council not to restrict his freedom; when he did so, he alleged that he had funds barely sufficient to cover his most elementary needs.[14]

This pathetic petition did not fundamentally change the council's decision, though it did lift the much-feared sentence of exile to Algiers. Unfortunately the ban on a return to the New World, which Cabeza de Vaca may have desired, continued in force. As we review the sequence of these events we never cease to marvel at Núñez's tenacity, even in the midst of these recurring vicissitudes. In answer to his petition, on 25 November 1551 the council decided to review once more the suit that had been brought against him. But in spite of this, and as in the previous case, severe restrictions were imposed on him. Neither he nor his representatives could have access to the documents that had served as a basis for the trial and that contained a list of all the accusations and allegations against him. Amid these and other misfortunes Núñez—perhaps following the advice of Fernández de Oviedo—decided to bring out an edition of both his *Relación* and his *Comentarios;* it was published in Valladolid in 1555.

In the face of so many misfortunes, we can assume that Cabeza de Vaca dedicated a good part of his last energies to rewriting his manuscripts and perhaps to reading works about the New World that complemented those labors, works he could no doubt obtain in Valladolid, where he spent his last years. Cabeza de Vaca must have felt trapped in an enigmatic web of events and manipulations that seemed always to end in defeat. During those years of lonely and poverty-stricken old age his health failed for the first time. On 15 September 1556 the king granted him a small pension in the amount of 12,000 maravedises, a sum that Núñez requested to alleviate his poverty and enable him to seek medical attention. Enrique de Gandía and other scholars believe that Núñez died in Valladolid between 1556 and 1559, as a result of the illness alluded to in the warrant of 15 September 1556. We might well share this opinion, especially if we look at a little-known document, the *Verdadera relación de lo que sucedió al governador Jaime Rasquisa* by Alonso Gómez de Santaya, written after 1560. In it he tells us conclusively that Cabeza de Vaca "died in Valladolid, a very poor gentleman."[15] Among the many fictional accounts that continue to circulate are those asserting that Núñez obtained important posts at the end of his life and that he died amid honors and recognition. No matter how unpleasant it is to recognize the fact, the truth is quite otherwise. What does appear to be true is that Cabeza de Vaca, like Bernal Díaz del Castillo, the Inca Garcilaso, and other celebrated individuals of the time, eventually regarded his writings as the only possibility for genuine personal and historical justification. But what he could not foresee was that his brief *Relación* would hold a prominent place among the narratives recounting the discovery of the New World.[16] Nor could Cabeza de Vaca guess that the misfortunes awaiting him in the New World would in the end give him a deeper knowledge of himself and his gifts of leadership. If we read him with care, we may also conclude that the long series of misfortunes that he experienced on the arid plains of North America considerably refined his capacity for thought. His meditations on the deceits contained in "men's thoughts" (ch. XXXIV) confirm this enrichment of his inner life. I suspect that such inner discoveries often sustained Núñez when everything seemed to contradict his desires. And when he began his astonishing return to New Spain, the hope to disclose the failures of Pánfilo de Narváez's expedition must have motivated him.

The *Relación* has been said more than once to lack the refined writing style that we praise in the pages of López de Gómara, Antonio de Guevara, or the Inca Garcilaso. I believe that even a superficial reader can observe in Cabeza de Vaca's work detailed descriptions that remind us of the somber tones of medieval chronicles (for example, in chs. II and VII). Moreover, we will see that the construction of the narrative process often allows the interference of the fortuitous, of the many ambiguities that shade our interpretation of what really happened. But these peculiarities of the writing do not diminish the narrative's considerable importance. It is worth remembering that Núñez's tale begins without a textual frame of reference, and that it often assumes the difficult task of describing not only the unknown but also the doubts and uneasiness of a narrator who had shared the most primitive and brutal forms of human existence.

The chapter sequences of the *Relación* form five segments differentiated by their content and expositive rhythm. The first of these are the two chapters that recount the departure from Sanlúcar on 17 June 1527 and the arrival in Hispaniola and Cuba, as well as the expedition's prolonged stay on the latter island. The second part (end of ch. II to ch. VII) concentrates on events beginning with the landing in Florida and the sally made by Narváez's expedition to the village of Aute, in the northern part of the peninsula. In these chapters the forward dynamic and future plans of the conquering venture begin to fade. Working against an inhospitable environment, between the present-day cities of Tallahassee and Apalachicola, the Spaniards built boats to escape the brutal conditions around them and the almost constant fights with Indians. Once the boats or rafts were ready, they sailed westward in the direction of New Spain, hugging the coast, until a desperate series of shipwrecks scattered the company. In the third segment of the narrative (from ch. VII to ch. XV) the writer begins to relate the misfortunes suffered by the Spaniards on the Isle of Ill Fortune (Galveston Island). From there on, and now in a different tone, the narrative often becomes introspective and imprecise, perhaps because it reflects the long cycle of humiliations and isolation endured by the last four survivors of the expedition. This fourth stage of the narrative, the longest and most complex, concludes with ch. XXXIII. In the last five chapters—which constitute the fifth narrative segment—Cabeza de Vaca and his companions at last detect the welcome presence of Spanish troops operating in northern New Spain. The last portion ends the *Naufragios;* prominent in this last section are the two final chapters, for they recount the arrival of the survivors in New Spain, the unexpected prophecies of the Moorish woman of Hornachos, and also Núñez's slightly fictionalized return to Castile.

In its primary form, Cabeza de Vaca's text hews to the rhetorical precepts that governed the preparation of *relaciones.* But its paradoxical and extremely varied content goes far beyond the usual expositive scheme of the *relación.* The skillful prologue contains a rather broad range of clichés and formulas that remind us of different types of literary creations, as well as rhetorical codifications harking back to classical texts. Among others is the familiar *laudatio* to the monarch, a rhetorically institutionalized characterization of the king as the model of justice and faith. No less trite is the allusion to Fate as the basis of all doubtful endeavors. And an affectedly humble description of Núñez's writing reflects the formulas known in rhetoric as *mediocritas mea* and *excusatio propter infirmitatem.* We also observe that the language of the prologue corresponds to the familiar rhetorical propositions stated by one who brings "news never heard before." *El libro de Aleixandre* (1252), along with many later texts, begins with this well known rhetorical device.

Cabeza de Vaca's narrative is shaped by the autobiographical imperative to write history out of personal experience, a narrative projection that often reappears in important reports or histories of the sixteenth and seventeenth centuries. Like all narrative springing in part from an autobiographical aim, the past that is being recounted becomes more and more the narrator's past. Even without conscious intent, this type of writing frequently leads to a problematical rhetorical confluence between the historical individual and the narrator's imaginative view of himself.

If we try to offer an all-embracing description of the *Relación*, we must remember that in this text, as in every narrative with a partially autobiographical aspect, what is written not only sets down the events but also describes both directly and implicitly the production of what is narrated. This fact makes obvious the surreptitious self-reference of the writing in the *Relación*. The narrative took shape in a series of successive rewritings—beginning in 1527 and ending about 1554—in which the last version refers as much to the shape of the previous text as to the sequence of events described; this process introduces a gradual and inevitable dispersion of signifieds, as is characteristic of textual creations that display a process of successive narrative broadenings. And furthermore, this process affords great flexibility in the ordering of arguments, the structuring of what is recounted, and the choice of what is narrated. So as not to judge him arbitrarily, we must insist on the fact that Núñez's famous text illustrates a careful series of rewritings that apparently never achieved a final formulation. Expressed in other terms, the *Relación* has retained a sense of provisionality, almost of a first draft, which paradoxically brings us closer to its fundamental nature. In its problematized and inconclusive structure, not in its story of marine disaster, we find the most striking examples of anguish that the text has to offer. By describing it in these terms, I emphasize that we must read the last two chapters, embellished by the appearance of pirates and the astonishing prophecy of a seeress of Hornachos, with greater imaginative latitude, especially if we link it to clichés that enjoyed much literary popularity at the time in Mediterranean fiction.

Within this broader perspective, if the misfortunes endured by Narváez's expedition had been foretold by the seeress of Hornachos, we could read Núñez's *Relación*, first of all, as an example of prophetic discourse; this possibility clearly expands the text's imaginary dimension but also casts doubt on its historical content. These later twists in the narrative introduce clearly literary themes and motifs into the text. Through the seeress of Hornachos, the prophetic action so popular in Renaissance literature enters the picture. Moreover, there are battles with pirates, incidents that immediately bring to mind a vast Mediterranean narrative built around similar adventures that we recognize as a legacy of the Byzantine novel, always so fond of describing adventures connected with shipwrecks and rescues. We also know that the seeress of Hornachos herself is one of a long line that links her to Spain and the Camacha described by Cervantes in his "Coloquio de los perros" and links her to America and the Negro wise woman Juana García; this last is a figure who appears in Juan Rodríguez Freyle's *Carnero* (1937) and recalls the famous procuress in Fernando de Rojas's *Celestina* (1499). With these observations in mind, we easily comprehend why Cabeza de Vaca's *Relación* has in its turn inspired several fictional works. Among the most recent is *The New Argonautica* (1928) by Walter Brooks Henderson, as well as two works by John U. Terrell, *Journey into Darkness* (1962) and *Estevanico the Black* (1968). Of greater imaginative scope is Oakley Hall's novel *The Children of the Sun* (1983), also based on the adventures of Cabeza de Vaca. *El largo atardecer del Caminante* (1992) by Abel Posee is another novel based on the life of Cabeza de Vaca.

Because the text edited here often undertakes the primal task of naming the unknown, its naming action links Cabeza de Vaca's *Relación* to myth as well as to powerful imaginative writings represented today by Gabriel García Márquez's *One Hundred Years of Solitude* (1966) and Mario Vargas Llosa's *War of the End of the World* (1981). But by bringing up these comparisons I do not suggest that we view the *Relación* as a primary precursor of modern Latin American fiction today. We can state, however, that the narrative organization of Cabeza de Vaca's text displays a considerable imaginative content, as corroborated by recent readings of the *Relación* (see the bibliography). I believe that the fertile variety of its components is the quality that allows us to describe Núñez's text today as seminal to the Hispanoamerican narrative tradition.

CASTAWAYS

FIGURE 2.   Alvar Núñez Cabeza de Vaca (1491?–1559?). The provenance of this rare portrait is unknown. It was first identified by McGraw-Hill publishers.

PROLOGUE

To His Sacred, Caesarean, Catholic Majesty

Among all the princes who we know have existed in the world, I believe that none can be found whom men have tried to serve with such true willingness and so great diligence and desire, as we see that they offer to Your Majesty today.[1] And it can clearly be observed thereby that this is not without great cause and reason, nor are men so blind that all of them would follow this path unseeing and without foundation; for we see that not only those of your native country who are obliged by faith and obedience to do so, but even foreigners, strive to surpass them. But though all are agreed in desire and willingness to serve, quite apart from the advantage that each may take from it, there is a very great difference caused not by any fault of theirs, but only by Fate; rather, it is the fault of no one, but solely the will and judgment of God, from Whom comes the fact that one man ends with more important services than he intended, and that everything happens to another in so contrary a manner that he can show no witness for his desires other than his own zeal; and even this is so well concealed at times that it cannot be recognized.

Of myself I can say that during the journey I made on the continent, at Your Majesty's command, I truly felt that my deeds and services were as clear and manifest as those of my ancestors; and that I would have no need to speak in order to be counted among those who, with perfect faith and utmost diligence, administer and undertake Your Majesty's appointments and do them justice. But since neither my advice nor my best efforts sufficed to win what we had gone to accomplish in Your Majesty's service, and because God permitted, for our sins, that of all the fleets that have gone to these lands, none found themselves in such great dangers or had such a miserable and disastrous end, no opportunity was afforded me to perform more service than this, which is to bring Your Majesty an account of what I learned and saw in ten years during which I wandered lost and naked through many and very strange lands, as well as the location of the lands and provinces and their distances, their supplies of food and the animals that live there, and the diverse customs of many and very barbarous nations with whom I spoke and lived, and all the other details that I could learn and know that may in some wise be of service to Your Majesty; for although the hope I had of departing from amongst them was always very slight, I had always the greatest care and diligence to remember everything very particularly, so that if at some time God Our Lord would be pleased to bring me hither where I am now, my account could testify to my good will and be of service to Your Majesty. Since the report of it is, I believe, advice of no little use to those who in your name will go to conquer those lands and bring them to the knowledge of the true Faith and the true lordship and service of Your Majesty, I wrote it with great certainty that, though many new things are to be read in it, and things very difficult for some to believe, they may believe them without any doubt; and may fully believe that throughout I have made my account rather short than long, and suffice it to say that I have offered the account to Your Majesty as truth. And I entreat Your Majesty to receive it as a mark of service, for it is the only thing that a man who left those lands naked could bring out with him.

CHAPTER I

Which Recounts When the Fleet Sailed, and the Officers and Men Who Went in It

On the seventeenth of June in the year fifteen hundred and twenty-seven,[2] Governor Pánfilo de Narváez sailed from the port of Sanlúcar de Barrameda with authority and orders from Your Majesty to conquer and govern the provinces that lie between the river of Las Palmas and the tip of Florida, which are on the mainland. And the fleet that he commanded consisted of five ships, in which there were six hundred men more or less. The officers he took (for mention must be made of them) were those whose names follow: Cabeza de Vaca, as treasurer and chief officer of justice; Alonso Enríquez, auditor; Alonso de Solís, tax agent of Your Majesty; and as inspector there was a friar of the Order of Saint Francis, a commissary officer named Fray Juan Suárez, and four other friars belonging to the same order. We reached the island of Santo Domingo, where we remained for almost forty-five days, providing ourselves with some necessary things, especially horses. Here more than a hundred and forty of the men of our fleet were lost to us, for they decided to stay there, influenced by the offers and promises made to them by the folk of the island.

We sailed from Santo Domingo and reached Santiago, which is a port on the island of Cuba, where the governor, in the few days we stayed there, supplied himself further with men, arms, and horses. And there it chanced that a gentleman named Vasco Porcallo, a resident of the town of Trinidad on the same island, offered the governor certain supplies that he owned in Trinidad, which is a hundred leagues[3] from the aforesaid port of Santiago. The governor started thence with the whole fleet;

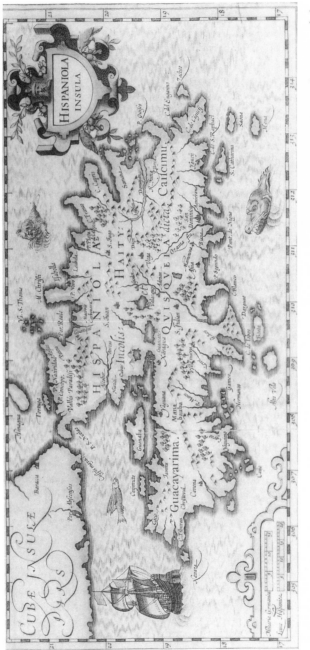

FIGURE 3. Map of Hispaniola, late sixteenth or early seventeenth century. Attributed to J. W. Blaeu. (Courtesy of the Hispanic Society of America)

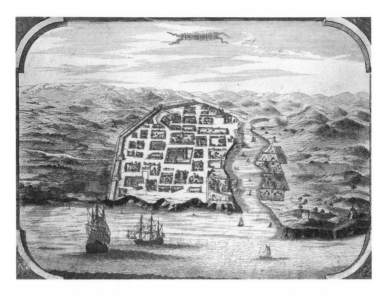

FIGURE 4.   View of Santo Domingo, ca. 1600. Engraving attributed to an anonymous Flemish painter. (Courtesy of the Hispanic Society of America)

but when we had reached a port called Cabo de Santa Cruz, which is halfway, he thought it best to wait there and send a ship to bring back those supplies; and for the purpose he ordered a certain Captain Pantoja to go there with his ship and commanded me to go with him in a second ship for safety's sake, while he stayed behind with four ships, for he had bought another in Santo Domingo. When Captain Pantoja arrived at the port of Trinidad with these two ships, he went with Vasco Porcallo to the town, a league's distance away, to receive the supplies. I stayed at sea with the pilots, who told us to finish our business there as speedily as possible, for that harbor was a very poor one and many ships were often lost there; and because what happened to us there was a matter of grave importance, I thought that it would not be out of place to recount it here, as part of my aim in writing of my travels.

Next morning the weather began to show signs of worsening,

for it started to rain and the sea became so rough that, though I gave the members of the crew leave to go ashore, when they saw how bad the weather was and that the town was a league away, many returned to the ship to avoid being exposed to the rain and cold. Just then a canoe came from the town, bringing me a letter from a resident of the place and beseeching me to go there, and offering to give me such supplies as they had and were needful for us; but I declined, saying that I could not leave the ships. At about noon the canoe returned with another letter, strongly urging the same, and they had brought a horse for me to ride. I gave the same reply as I had at first, saying that I would not leave the ships; but the pilot and crew importuned me to go, to hasten to bring the supplies as soon as possible so that we could leave quickly, for they greatly feared that the ships would be lost if they stayed there for long.

For this reason I determined to go to the town, though before leaving I gave orders to the pilots that if the wind began to blow from the south, which in that part of the world often causes ships to be lost, and they saw themselves in great danger, they should drive the ships onshore in a place where the men and horses would be saved. And upon this I departed; and though I wanted to take some men with me for company they refused to go, saying that it was raining hard, and cold, and the town was very far away; that next day, which was Sunday, with God's help they would go to attend mass. An hour after I had gone ashore the sea became very violent, and the north wind blew so hard that even the ships' boats dared not make for shore, nor could they drive the ships onshore by any means, for there was an offshore wind; so that by dint of great effort, with two contrary winds and heavy rain, they stayed there all that day and all of Sunday until nightfall.

At that hour the rain and wind began to increase so much that the storm was no less severe in the town than upon the sea, for all the houses and churches were blown down, and seven or eight of us had to walk with arms linked to prevent the wind from carrying us away; and as we walked among trees we were no less frightened, fearing that, as they were falling too, we would be killed underneath them. We spent the whole night in the storm and in this danger, without finding a single place or spot where we could be safe for half an hour at a time. And meanwhile we heard all night long, especially after midnight, a mighty crashing and sound of voices, and loud sounds of bells and flutes and tambourines and other instruments, which lasted until morning when the storm abated. Nothing so fearful had ever been seen in these parts; I collected testimony concerning it, an official report of which I sent to Your Majesty. On Monday morning we went down to the port and did not find the ships; we saw their buoys in the water, whence we realized that they were lost; and we went along the coast to see whether we could find any trace of them. And as we found none we moved inland and, searching there, a quarter of a league from the water, we found a ship's boat up in some trees, and ten leagues along the coast we found two crewmen from my ship and a few tops of boxes; and the bodies were so disfigured by being dashed against the rocks that they were unrecognizable. We also found a cape and a shredded coverlet, and nothing else appeared.

Sixty men and twenty horses were lost in the ships. Those who had gone ashore on the day that they arrived, some thirty, were all that were left of those who had been in both ships. Thus we suffered great trials and hunger for several days, because the supplies and subsistence that the town possessed had been lost, and some livestock, and the land was in such a state that it was pitiful to see: trees fallen, forests stripped bare, all without foliage or grass. In this plight we spent five days in the month of November, when the governor arrived with his four ships, which had also passed through a great storm and had escaped by taking timely refuge in a safe place. The crews that came in them, as well as those already there, were so terrified by what had happened that they greatly feared taking ship in winter and implored the governor to spend the season there. And he, perceiving that they and the residents of the town wished it, decided to winter there. He placed me in charge of the ships and crews, to go with them to winter in the port of Jagua, which is twelve leagues distant from there, and where I stayed until the twentieth day of February.

CHAPTER II

How the Governor Arrived at the Port of Jagua and Brought a Pilot with Him

At this time the governor arrived there with a brigantine that he had bought in Trinidad and brought with him a pilot named Miruelo, whom he had hired because he said that he was familiar with the river of Las Palmas[4] and had been there and was a very good pilot for the whole northern coast. The governor had also bought a ship and left it on the coast of Havana, placing Alvaro de la Cerda in it as captain with forty men and twelve horses; and two days after the governor's arrival we set sail, and the crews we carried consisted of four hundred men and eighty horses in four ships and a brigantine. The pilot whom we had again engaged steered the ships through the shoals known as Canarreos, so that on the second day we went aground and like this, with the keels of the ships often touching bottom, we spent two weeks, at the end of which a storm from the south brought so much water into the shoals that we were able to get out of them, though not without great danger.

When we had left there and reached Guaniguanico, another storm caught us and we were almost shipwrecked. On Cape Corrientes we had another, where we spent three days. After these storms we rounded Cape San Antonio[5] and sailed, in bad weather, until we were within twelve leagues of Havana; and on the next day, when we were preparing to enter the harbor, a storm came up from the south that drove us offshore and we crossed over to the coast of Florida and reached land on Tuesday, the twelfth of April; and we sailed along the coast of Florida, and on Maundy Thursday, on the same coast, we sailed into the mouth of a bay,[6] at the tip of which we saw certain Indian houses and huts.

CHAPTER III

How We Reached Florida

On this same day the auditor Alonso Enríquez left the ship and went ashore on an island that is in that bay and called to the Indians, who came and spent a good space of time with him and gave him fish and a few pieces of venison by way of barter. On the following day, which was Good Friday, the governor disembarked with as many crewmen as he could take in the ships' boats, and when we reached the Indian huts or houses that we had seen we found them abandoned and empty, for the people had gone away that night in their canoes. One of those huts was very large, for it could hold more than three hundred persons; the others were smaller, and we found a gold rattle there among the fishnets. On the following day the governor raised banners for Your Majesty and took possession of the land in your royal name, and presented his credentials and was received as governor, as Your Majesty commanded.

We also presented our credentials to him, and he accepted them as their contents instructed him to do. Then he ordered the rest of the people to disembark, along with the remaining horses, of which there were only forty-two, for the others had perished as a result of the great storms and long time they had spent at sea; and the few who remained were so thin and exhausted that for the present we could make very little use of them. On the following day the Indians from that village came to see us, and though they spoke to us we did not understand them, for we had no interpreter; but they made many signs and threatening gestures, and we thought they were telling us to leave their land; and on this they left us alone, without interfering with us in any way, and departed.

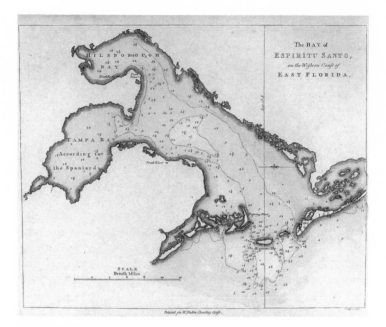

FIGURE 5. Tampa Bay. [Eighteenth century?] Area where Pánfilo de Narváez's expedition landed in 1528. (Courtesy of the Florida Historical Society)

CHAPTER IV

How We Marched Inland

Two days later the governor decided to march into the interior, to explore it and see what was there. The commissary and the inspector and I went with him, with forty men of whom six were riding horses, though we could make little use of them. We marched in a northerly direction until, at the hour of vespers, we reached a very large bay, which we thought extended deeply into the land; we stayed there that night and next day returned to where the ships and crews were. The governor ordered the brigantine to sail along the coast of Florida and seek the harbor that Miruelo the pilot had said that he knew about; but he had already missed it, and did not know where we were or where the harbor was; and the brigantine was ordered, if it were not found, to cross to Havana and seek out the ship that Alvaro de la Cerda was commanding, and after having taken on some provisions it was to come back and look for us. After the brigantine had left, the same party as before, with a few additional men, again marched inland and followed the shore of the bay we had found; and when we had marched for four leagues we seized four Indians and showed them maize to see if they recognized it, for until then we had seen no sign of it. They told us that they would lead us where there was some maize, and so they took us to their village, which is at the end of the bay near there, and in the village they showed us a little maize that was not yet ready to pick.

There we found many cases belonging to traders from Castile, and in each one was the body of a dead man, the bodies covered with painted deerskins. The commissary thought that this was some kind of idolatry and burned the cases along with the bodies. We also found pieces of canvas and cloth, and feathered headdresses that appeared to be from New Spain.

13

We also found small amounts of gold. We asked the Indians by signs where those things had come from. They indicated to us that very far away was a province called Apalachee,[7] where there was much gold, and made signs indicating that there was a large quantity of everything we wanted. They said that there was great abundance in Apalachee, and so we left that place, taking those Indians with us as guides; and when we had marched for ten or twelve leagues we found another village of fifteen houses, where there was a good stand of maize growing, almost ready to cut, and we also found some maize that was already dry. And after we had spent two days there we returned to where the auditor and the men and ships were and told the auditor and pilots what we had seen and the information the Indians had given us; the next day, which was the first of May, the governor called the commissary and the auditor and the inspector and me to one side, along with a sailor named Bartolomé Fernández and a scribe named Jerónimo de Alaniz, and when we were assembled he told us that he wanted to explore inland, and that the ships should follow the coast until they reached the harbor, and that the pilots said and believed that by sailing in the direction of Las Palmas they would be very close to it; and he asked our opinion about this.

I replied that I thought we should by no means leave the ships until they were first settled in a safe harbor where there were people, and that he should consider that the pilots were not sure of themselves, nor did they agree with each other, nor did they know where they were, and that besides this the horses were in no condition to be of use to us in any need that might arise; and that in addition to this, we were powerless to speak without an interpreter, so that we could not understand the Indians nor could they know what we wanted in the land, and that we were going into a land we knew nothing about, nor what it was like, nor what was in it, nor what kind of people lived in it, nor in what part of it we were, and that in addition to all this we did not have supplies sufficient to go into a place we did not know. For in view of the provisions the ships were carrying, we could give each man no more than a ration of a pound of ship's biscuit and another of salt pork for the journey inland, and that in my opinion we ought to reembark and search for a harbor and land that would be more suitable for colonization, for what we had seen was as thinly settled and poor as had ever been found in those parts. The commissary's opinion was just the opposite, saying that we ought not to embark, but that by constantly following the coast the ships should search for the harbor, for the pilots said that the coast of Pánuco was probably only ten or fifteen leagues away,[8] and that it was impossible, if we always followed the coast, not to hit upon it, because the pilots said that it penetrated into the land for twelve leagues, and that the first party to find it should wait there for the others, and that to put to sea was to tempt God. For ever since we left Castile we had suffered great difficulties: we had been through so many storms, so many losses of ships and men before arriving there; and that for these reasons he thought we should march along the coast until we reached the harbor, and that the other ships with the rest of the men should go the same way until they reached the same harbor. Everyone who was there thought that this was the best thing to do, except for the scribe, who said that rather than leave the ships unprotected they ought to be left in a known and safe harbor, in a place that was populated: that once this had been done the governor could march inland and do whatever seemed best to him.

The governor followed his own inclinations and the advice of the others; seeing his determination, I adjured him in Your Majesty's name not to leave the ships unless they were in a harbor and safe, and requested it in writing through the scribe that we had with us. He answered that, since he was in agreement with the opinion of the majority of the other officers and the commissary, I had no right to make these demands of him. And he asked the scribe to write in the record that, because there were not sufficient food supplies in that place to establish a colony, nor a harbor for the ships, he was breaking up the settlement that he had established there and going to look for a better harbor and better land. And then he ordered those who were to go with him to get ready, to prepare everything needful for the journey. And after all was ready, in the presence of all those who were there, he told me that because I had made so much trouble and feared going inland, I should stay there and take charge of the ships and the crews who remained in them, and set up a settlement if I arrived before him. I refused to do this.

After we left there, on that same afternoon, saying that he believed he could not trust anyone else to do it, he sent a message to say that he begged me to undertake the duty. And, seeing that even though he insisted so urgently I continued to refuse, he asked me why I was reluctant to accept? To which I replied that I did not want to accept that duty because I felt certain, and was convinced, that he would never see the ships again, nor the ships him, and that I believed this because I could see how ill equipped they were for starting inland, and that I preferred to run the risks that they were running and endure what he and they were enduring, rather than take charge of the ships and let it be said that, because I had objected to the expedition inland, I had stayed behind out of fear, and that my honor would be impugned; and that I preferred to risk my life rather than place my honor in that position. The governor, seeing that he could not persuade me, asked many others to speak to me about it and beg me to do it, to whom I replied as I had to him; and so he appointed as his lieutenant, to stay with the ships, an officer named Caravallo who had come with him.

CHAPTER V

How the Governor Left the Ships

On Saturday the first of May, the same day that this had happened, the governor ordered two pounds of ship's biscuit and half a pound of salt pork to be issued to each of the men who were to go with him, and so we set off inland. The total number of people that we had was three hundred men: among them were the commissary Fray Juan Suárez and another friar named Fray Juan de Palos, and three priests and the officers. Those of us who were mounted consisted of forty men, and we marched with the supplies we had brought for two weeks, without finding anything else to eat except palm hearts like those of Andalusia. During this whole time we did not encounter a single Indian, nor did we see a house or village, and at last we reached a river that we crossed with great difficulty, swimming and on rafts; we spent a whole day crossing it, for it had a very swift current. After we had reached the other side some two hundred Indians, more or less, came to meet us; the governor went toward them, and after he conversed with them by signs they gestured toward us in such a way that it became necessary to confront them; and we took five or six of them captive, and these took us to their houses, which were about half a league from there, where we found a large quantity of maize ready for harvesting. And we gave infinite thanks to Our Lord for having aided us in so great a need, for indeed, since we were new to misfortune, in addition to being very tired we were faint with hunger; and on the third day after our arrival there, the auditor and the inspector and the commissary and I joined together and implored the governor to send a party to look for the sea, to find out if we could discover a harbor, for the Indians said that the sea was not far off.

He replied that it was useless for us to speak about that, for

FIGURE 6.   View of the west coast of Florida as it must have looked
to the Narváez expedition. Photo ca. 1860. (Courtesy of the Florida
Historical Society)

it was very far away. And because I was the one who was
most insistent, he told me to go and find it and look for a
harbor, and to go on foot with forty men; and so next day I
set off with Captain Alonso del Castillo and forty men from
his company; and we marched until about noon and reached
some shallows of the sea that seemed to extend far into the
land. We walked over them for a league and one-half with
water up to the middle of our thighs, stepping on oysters,
which gave us many severe cuts on our feet and caused us a
great deal of trouble, until we reached the river we had crossed
at first, which entered into that same bay. And since we could
not cross it because we were ill prepared to do so, we returned
to camp and told the governor what we had found and how
we would have to cross the river again in the same place where
we had passed it at first, so as to explore that bay thoroughly
and see if there was a harbor there; the next day he sent a
captain named Valenzuela to cross the river with sixty men
and six horses, and to march down it until they reached the
sea and to see if there was a harbor. After being there for two
days, he returned and said that he had discovered the inlet

and that it was all shallow bay and only knee-deep, and that there was no harbor, and that he had seen five or six canoes of Indians who crossed from one side to the other and were wearing headdresses of many feathers.

Having learned this, we left the place next day, always marching toward that province that the Indians had called Apalachee, taking as guides those whom we had captured; and we marched in this manner until the seventeenth of June and found no Indians who dared to confront us. And then a chief, carried on the back of another Indian and covered with a painted deerskin, came to meet us; he brought many people with him, and some walked before him playing on reed flutes; and he reached the place where the governor was and spent an hour with him, and we gave him to understand by signs that we were going to Apalachee; and according to the signs[9] that he made, it appeared that he was an enemy of the men of Apalachee and would help us to go against it. We gave him beads and hawk's bells and other barter goods, and he gave the governor the skin that covered him, and then he turned back and we followed after him in the direction he was going. That night we reached a river, which was very deep and wide and had a strong current, and because we dared not cross it on rafts we made a canoe for the purpose. We spent a whole day crossing it, and if the Indians had wished to attack us they could easily have prevented us from crossing, and even with their help we had great difficulty. One of the mounted men, Juan Velázquez by name, a native of Cuéllar, did not want to wait and entered the river, and as the current was swift it knocked him off his horse, and he clung to the reins and he and the horse were drowned; and the Indians belonging to that chief, who was called Dulchanchellín, found the horse and told us where we would find him down the river, and so they went to fetch him, and his death caused us great grief because until then we had not lost a man.

The horse provided supper for many men that night. Having crossed the river, next day we reached the village of that chief and he sent us maize. When the men went to get water that night, they shot arrows at one of us Spaniards, and by God's will he was not wounded. Next day we left there without any of the native Indians making an appearance, for all of them had fled, but as we marched Indians appeared, coming with warlike intent, and though we called to them, they refused to turn around or confront us; rather, they fell back and followed us in the same direction we were traveling. The governor laid an ambush on the path, using several of the mounted men, who attacked them as they passed and captured three or four Indians whom we used as guides from then on. They led us through terrain that was very difficult to traverse and wonderful to see, for there are great woods there and marvelously tall trees; and there were so many fallen trees on the ground that they barred our way, so thoroughly that we could not get through them except by going a long way around them, and with great difficulty; and of those that had not fallen, many were split from top to bottom from the lightning that strikes in that part of the world, where there are constantly great storms and tempests.

We marched with these difficulties until the day after the feast of Saint John, when we came in sight of Apalachee without the knowledge of the Indians of that land; we offered many thanks to God when we saw that we were so close to it, believing that what we had been told about that land was true, that it would be the end of the great hardship we had endured, both because of the long and hard march we had made and the great hunger we had suffered; for though sometimes we found maize, most times we marched for seven or eight leagues without chancing upon any; and there were many among us who, besides great fatigue and hunger, had sores on their backs from carrying their weapons in addition to the other things they had to carry. But when we saw that we had arrived at the place we desired, and where they had told us there was such abundance and gold, it seemed to us that a large part of our weariness and hunger had been lifted from us.

CHAPTER VI

How We Reached Apalachee

When we had arrived within sight of Apalachee,[10] the governor ordered me to take nine men on horseback and fifty on foot and enter the town, and the inspector and I did this; and when we entered it we found only women and children, for the men were not in the town at the time. But a short time later, as we walked about, they returned and began to attack us, shooting arrows at us and killing the inspector's horse; but at last they fled and left us alone. We found a large quantity of maize there that was ready to harvest, and much dry maize that they had stored. We found many deerskins, and among them a few of the woven blankets, though small and not of good quality, that the women use to cover part of their persons. They had many vessels to grind maize. There were some forty small houses in the town, built low and in sheltered places for fear of the great storms that are constant in that land. Their buildings are of straw, and they are surrounded by very thick woods and great stands of trees and many swamps, where there are so many large fallen trees that they are a hindrance, and the reason why that land cannot be traversed without a great deal of effort and danger.

CHAPTER VII

Of the Manner of the Land

The land is level, for the most part, from the place where we disembarked to this town and land of Apalachee: the ground is sand and also loam; everywhere there are large trees and clearings in which there are walnut trees and bay trees and others of the kind called gum trees, cedars, junipers and holm oaks and pines and oak trees, and low palmettos like those of Castile. Throughout the land are many large and small lakes, some very difficult to cross, in part because they are very deep and in part because there are so many fallen trees in them. Their bottoms are sandy, and those in the neighborhood of Apalachee are larger than those we saw on the way. There are many fields of maize in this province, and the houses are scattered over the countryside just as they are in Gelves.[11] The animals we saw there are three kinds of deer, rabbits and hares, bears and lions and other wild beasts; among them we saw an animal that carries its young in a pouch on its belly, and during all the time they are small it carries them there until they know how to forage for themselves, and if they happen to be outside looking for food and people approach, the mother does not run away until she has gathered them into her pouch.

The land in those parts is very cold: it has very good grazing for livestock; there are many kinds of birds; many geese, ducks, teal, mallards, ibis, egrets, herons, partridges: we saw numbers of hawks, peregrine falcons, sparrow hawks, pigeon hawks, and many other birds. Two hours after we reached Apalachee, the Indians who had fled on our approach returned with peaceful intent, asking us for their women and children, and we returned them, except that the governor kept one of their chiefs with him, which offended them greatly; and next day they returned ready for war and attacked us so fiercely and rapidly

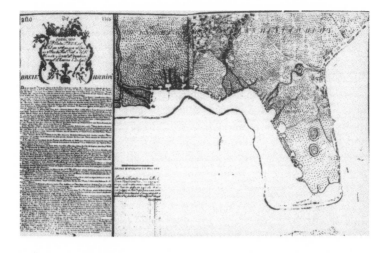

FIGURE 7.   Map of the provinces of Florida. By D. Juan Joseph Elixio de la Puente, 1768. Geographic Service of the Spanish Army. (Courtesy of the Florida Historical Society)

that they succeeded in setting fire to the houses we were in: but when we came out they fled and retreated to the lakes that were nearby; and for this reason, and because of the large fields of maize, we were not able to do them harm except for one whom we killed. Next day other Indians from another village in the opposite direction came and attacked us in the same way as the others and escaped in the same manner, and one of them was also killed. We stayed in this town for twenty-five days, during which we made three sallies into the countryside and found it very thinly populated and hard to march in because of the difficult trails and woods and lakes that were there.

We asked the chief whom we had captured from them, along with the other Indians we had brought with us, who lived not far from them and were their enemies, what the land and its people were like, and how well supplied it was and everything else about it. Each replied separately that the largest town in all that land was Apalachee, and that farther on there were fewer people and much poorer than they were, and that the land was sparsely settled and its inhabitants very scattered; and that if we went forward there were great lakes and thick woods and large deserts and empty spaces. Then we asked about the land to the south, what towns and resources did it have? They said that in that direction, nine days' journey toward the sea, there was a town that they called Aute,[12] and that the Indians there had much maize and that they had beans and pumpkins, and because it was so close to the sea they were able to catch fish, and that these Indians were friends of theirs. In view of the poverty of the land and the unfavorable information they gave us about the inhabitants and everything else, and as the Indians made war on us continually, wounding our people and horses at the places where we went to get water; and as they did this from the lakes, and so well protected that we could not retaliate, because they shot arrows at us from the lakes and killed a man from Texcoco named Don Pedro, whom the commissary had brought with him, we decided to leave there and go in search of the sea and that town of Aute they had told us of; and so we left there twenty-five days after we had arrived.

On the first day we traversed those lakes and trails without seeing a single Indian; but on the second day we reached a lake that was very hard to cross because the water came up to our chests and there were many fallen tree trunks in it. And when we were in the middle of it we were attacked by many Indians who had been hiding behind some trees so that we could not see them: others were on fallen trees and began to shoot arrows at us, so that they wounded many men and horses and captured the guide we had with us before we could emerge from the lake; and after we had left it they followed us again, trying to stop us, so that we were unable to leave the lake behind or concentrate our forces and try to fight them, for then they entered the lake and wounded our men and horses from there. In view of this the governor ordered the horsemen to dismount and attack them on foot. The auditor dismounted with them, and they attacked the Indians and they all fought together in the lake, and so we forced our way through. In this affray some of our men were wounded, and the good weapons they carried were of no use; and there were men that day who swore they had seen two oak trees, each as thick as the lower part of a man's leg, shot clear through by the Indians' arrows. And this is not so much to be wondered at considering the strength and skill with which they shoot them, for I myself saw an arrow at the foot of a poplar tree that had penetrated into it two handbreadths. All the Indians that we saw, from Florida to here, use arrows; and as they are so tall and go about naked, they look like giants when seen from a distance. They are wonderfully handsome folk, very lean and extremely strong and agile. The bows they use are as thick as a man's arm and eleven or twelve handbreadths long, which they shoot at a distance of two hundred paces, so surely that they never miss anything. After we had made this crossing, a league farther on we came to another that was very like it, except for the fact that, as it was half a league wide, it was much worse; this one we crossed without hindrance and without attacks by Indians, for as they had used up all their supplies of arrows in the first encounter, they had nothing left with which they dared to confront us. On the following day, as we made another similar crossing, I found traces of people who had gone ahead of us and warned the governor of it, for he was in the rear guard: and so, although the Indians attacked us, they were unable to harm us because we were forewarned, and when we emerged on level ground they continued to follow us. We attacked them on two sides and killed two Indians, and they wounded me and two or three other Spaniards, and because they took shelter in the woods we were unable to do them any more harm or damage. We marched like this for eight days, and after the crossing I have described no more Indians attacked us until a league farther on, which is the place that, as I have said, we were going.

As we were going our way, Indians came out of the woods without our hearing them and attacked the rear guard, and among them was a hidalgo named Avellaneda who turned around on hearing the cries of a lad who was a servant of his and went to his aid, and the Indians hit him with an arrow at the edge of his cuirass, and the wound was so severe that almost all the arrow went into his neck and he died on the spot, and we carried him to Aute. We arrived after nine days of journeying from Apalachee, and when we reached there we found all the people fled, and the houses burned, and a great quantity of maize and pumpkins and beans, all ready to be harvested. We rested there for two days, and after that the governor asked me to go and find the sea, for the Indians said it was very close by: during this journey we thought we had discovered it because of a very large river that we found, which we named the Magdalena. In view of this, on the next day I set off to find it, along with the commissary and Captain Castillo and Andrés Dorantes and seven other mounted men and fifty on foot, and we marched until the hour of vespers, when we reached an inlet or arm of the sea where we found many oysters, which the men enjoyed greatly, and we gave great thanks to God for having brought us there.

Next morning I sent twenty men to explore the coast and find out what it was like; they returned on the following night saying that those inlets and bays were very large and entered so deeply into the land that they made it extremely difficult to find out what we wished to know, and that the coast was very far away. Once we had learned this, and considering the fact that we were ill prepared and ill equipped to explore the coast, I returned to the governor. When we arrived we found him and many others sick, and the previous night the Indians had come upon them and placed them in great peril owing to the illness they had suffered; also, one of the horses had died. I reported to him what I had done, and the unfavorable lie of the land. That day we stayed there.

CHAPTER VIII

How We Departed from Aute

On the following day we departed from Aute and marched all day until we reached the place where I had been. The journey was extremely laborious, for there were not enough horses to carry the men who were sick, nor did we know what cure to apply, for they grew worse every day; and it was a very pitiable and painful thing to see the deprivation and hardship we were undergoing. When we had arrived we saw how little possibility we had of going forward, for there was nowhere to go, and even if the men had wished to continue they could not, for most of them were sick and in such a condition that there were few who could be of any use. I will not dwell on this here, for everyone can imagine what it was like to be in such a strange and evil land and without any possibility of help, either to stay or to leave; but since the surest help is God Our Lord, and we never lost faith in Him, something else occurred that made our situation even more desperate: most of the horsemen began to steal away, in the belief that they could find some recourse for themselves and abandon the governor and the invalids, who were absolutely weak and powerless.

But as there were many nobles and men of good family among them, they refused to allow this to happen without reporting it to the governor and Your Majesty's officers; and as we reproached them for their intentions and reminded them of the plight in which they were leaving their captain and those who were ill and powerless, and, in particular, for leaving Your Majesty's service, they agreed that they would remain and that the fate of one would be that of all, and that none would abandon another. When the governor saw this, he called all of them together and each man separately and asked their advice about this evil land and how to get out of it and find some help, since there was no help there; a third of our people were very ill, and since sickness was increasing by the hour, we were sure that all of us were going to succumb to it: hence nothing could follow but death, which was all the more to be feared being in the place where we were. And in view of this and many other difficulties, and having discussed many remedies, we agreed upon one that was extremely difficult to put into practice; and that was, to build boats in which to escape.

Everyone thought it impossible, for we did not know how to make them nor have tools, nor iron, nor forge, nor tow, nor pitch, nor rigging; in a word, not one of the many things that were needful, nor anyone who knew anything about accomplishing it, and especially we had no means of getting food while the boats were being built and feeding those who would do the work, in the way that we had agreed. And in consideration of all this we decided to think it over at more leisure, and the talk ceased for that day, and each man went away trusting to God Our Lord to lead him to where His will might be done. Next day God willed that one of our company came and said that he would make some wooden tubes, and that bellows could be made with deerskins; and as we were at a point when anything that offered some chance of help seemed good to us, we told him to start to do it, and we decided to make nails and saws and axes and other tools that were so badly needed out of the stirrups and spurs and crossbows and other articles of iron that we had on hand; and to provide food during the time this was being done, we determined that four sallies should be made to Aute with all the horses and men who were capable of going, and that every third day a horse should be killed, which would be shared among those who were working on the building of the boats and those who were ill; the sallies were made with the men and horses that were able to go, and in these expeditions they brought four hundred *fanegas*[13] of maize, though not without struggles and disputes with the Indians.

We gathered many palmettos in order to utilize their fiber and husks, twisting and preparing it to use in the boats in place of tow; construction of these began with the only ship's car-

FIGURE 8. Narváez's men build boats near Apalachicola, Florida. Drawing by Ettore De Grazia. (Courtesy of the De Grazia Art and Cultural Foundation)

penter in the company, and we worked so eagerly, beginning on the fourth day of August, that by the twentieth of September five boats were finished, each twenty-two cubits long, caulked with the palmetto fiber, and we tarred them with a kind of tarry pitch made by a Greek, Don Teodoro, from pine trees; and from the same palmetto fiber and the tails and manes of the horses we made cords and rigging, and sails out of our shirts, and from the juniper trees that grew there we made the oars that we believed we needed. And such was the land to which, for our sins, we had come that we had very great difficulty in finding stones to serve as ballast and anchors for the boats, for we had seen none anywhere. We also flayed the legs of the horses whole and tanned the hide to make bottles to carry water in.

During this time some of the men went to gather shellfish in the coves and inlets of the sea, where the Indians attacked them twice and killed ten men in full view of the camp, without our being able to come to their aid; we found them shot right through the body with arrows, for even though some had good weapons they were not sufficient to prevent this from happening, because the Indians shot their arrows with the skill and strength I have described before. And according to the sworn testimony of our pilots, from the bay we named Bay of the Cross to this point we had marched two hundred and eighty leagues, more or less; in all that land we never saw mountains, nor did we hear of them in any way; and before we embarked more than forty men died of illness and hunger in addition to those the Indians killed. On the twenty-second day of September we ate the last of the horses, for only one was left, and on that day we embarked in the following order: in the governor's boat were forty-nine men. In another, which he entrusted to the auditor and commissary, were an equal number. The third he gave to Captain Alonso del Castillo and Andrés Dorantes, with forty-eight men, and another to two captains named Téllez and Peñalosa, with forty-seven men. Command of the other he gave to the inspector and me, with forty-nine men, and after we had loaded our supplies and clothing scarcely a handbreadth of freeboard remained above the water, and in addition to this we were so crowded together that we could not move; and thus powerful was the need that made us dare to set out in this manner and embark upon so inclement a sea, with none among us having any knowledge of the art of navigation.

CHAPTER IX

How We Departed
from the Bay of Horses

The bay we left from is called the Bay of Horses,[14] and we sailed for seven days among those inlets, in waist-deep water, with no signs at all of any coast, and after emerging from them we reached an island that was near the land. My boat was ahead of the others, and we saw coming from the island five canoes of Indians, who abandoned them and left them in our possession when they saw that we were heading toward them. The other boats continued and discovered some houses on that island, where we found a large quantity of dried mullet and their eggs, which were a great help to us in our need. After we had eaten them we went on, and two leagues from there crossed a strait formed by the island and the mainland, to which we gave the name of Saint Michael because we had found it on his feast day, and after coming out of it we reached the coast, where we repaired the boats somewhat with the five canoes that I had captured from the Indians, making planks of them and adding them in such a way as to have two hand-breadths more of freeboard above the water.

This done, we again sailed along the coast in the direction of the river of Las Palmas, our thirst and hunger increasing daily, for our supplies were very scanty and we were nearly at the end of them; and we ran short of water because the skins we had made from the horses' legs soon rotted and were of no use; sometimes we came into coves and bays that penetrated very far inland; all of them were shallow and dangerous. And we continued in this way for thirty days, where occasionally we found Indian fishermen, poor and wretched folk. At the end of these thirty days, when our need of water was very great, one night as we sailed very near the coast we heard a canoe approaching, and when we saw it we waited until it approached, and it refused to come near us, and though we called to it, it did not turn around or wait for us; and because it was night we did not pursue it and continued on our way. When dawn came we saw a small island and went to it to see if we could find water, but our efforts were in vain, for none was there. While we were anchored there a very great storm overtook us, which caused us to stay there for six days, unable to put to sea; and as we had drunk nothing for five days, our thirst was so great that we had to drink salt water, and the wits of some were so disturbed by it that five men suddenly died.

I tell this so briefly because I believe that there is no need to recount details of the miseries and hardships in which we found ourselves, for considering the place we were in and the little hope of aid that we had, everyone can easily imagine what we suffered there. And as we saw that our thirst was increasing and the water was killing us, though the storm had not ceased we agreed to commend ourselves to God Our Lord and risk the dangers of the sea rather than await the certainty of death from thirst: and so we set off in the direction we had seen the canoe the night that we had arrived there. And that day we were so often on the point of foundering and being lost that there was not a man among us who did not think death certain. It pleased Our Lord, who often shows His favor in the greatest need, that at sunset we rounded a point of land where we found fair weather and shelter. Many canoes came toward us, and the Indians who had come in them spoke to us and then turned around without waiting for us. They were tall and handsome folk and did not carry arrows or bows. We followed them to their houses, which were nearby on a spit of land, and we went ashore and in front of the houses found many jars of water and a large quantity of cooked fish, and the chief of that region offered all of it to the governor and, taking him with him, carried him off to his house.

The houses of these Indians were made of reed mats and appeared to be fixed dwellings. After we entered the chief's house he gave us a great quantity of fish, and we gave him the maize we had with us, and the people ate it in our presence and asked for more and we gave it to them; and the governor gave him much barter goods. At midnight when the governor was in the chief's house, the Indians suddenly attacked us and the men who were very ill, who were lying on the sand; and they also attacked the chief's house where the governor was and wounded him in the face with a stone. The men who were there seized the chief, but as his people were so close by he slipped out of their hands and left behind a mantle made of sables, which are the best to be found in the world, I believe, and they have an odor that seems to be compounded of ambergris and musk and can be smelled at a great distance: we saw other furs there, but none were as fine as these.

Those of us who were nearby, seeing that the governor was wounded, got him into the boat and succeeded in embarking all the rest of the men into their boats; and about fifty of us stayed on land to defend ourselves from the Indians, who attacked us three times that night, and so fiercely that each time we had to fall back more than a stone's throw; not one among us but was wounded, and I received a wound in the face; and if they had possessed more arrows (for very few were found), no doubt they would have done us great harm. The third time they attacked, Captains Dorantes and Peñalosa and Téllez ambushed them with fifteen men and attacked them from behind and caused them to flee in such numbers that they left us alone. Next morning I broke up thirty of their canoes, which served as shelter from a north wind that was blowing, and we had to stay there all day suffering greatly from the cold, not daring to put to sea because of the great storm that was raging there. When it had passed we again took to the boats and sailed for three days, and as we had taken on little water and the vessels we had to carry it in were also few, we were again in very great need; and continuing on our way we entered an estuary, and while there we saw a canoe full of Indians approaching; as we hailed them, they came toward us, and the governor, whose boat they had reached first, asked them for water, and they offered it to us if we would give them the vessels in which we carried it; and one of the Christians, a Greek named Doroteo Teodoro, whom I have mentioned before, said that he wanted to go with them. The governor and others tried as hard as they could to prevent him but were unsuccessful, for he wanted to go with them in any case, and so he went and took a black with him, and the Indians left two of their company as hostages; and that night the Indians returned and brought back our vessels empty and did not bring the Christians they had taken with them; and as for those who had been left with us as hostages, while the others were talking to them they tried to jump into the water. But the men who were in the boat prevented them, and so the Indians fled in their canoe and left us very perplexed and sad, because we had lost those two Christians.

CHAPTER X

Of the Fight We Had with the Indians

In the morning many canoes full of Indians came to us, asking for the two men of their number who had stayed in the boat as hostages. The governor said that he would give them up if they would bring the two Christians that they had taken away. Five or six chiefs came with these people, and they seemed the handsomest, and those with most authority and sense of order that we had seen until now, though they were not as tall as the ones we have told about. They wore their hair loose and very long and were covered with cloaks made of sable skins like those we had taken before, and some of them were very curiously made, for sewed onto them were loops of hide resembling lion skin that looked very fine. They entreated us to go with them and said that they would give us the Christians and water and many other things; and many canoes continually approached us, trying to cut off the mouth of that inlet, and for this reason as well as the fact that the dry land was very dangerous, we put out to sea, where we stayed with the Indians until midday.

And as they refused to give us the Christians, and in consequence we did not give them the Indians, they began to fire stones at us with slings, and threw sticks and made gestures as if to shoot arrows at us, though we saw no more than three or four bows among them. While we were engaged in this fight the wind freshened and they turned about and left us, and so we sailed on that day until the hour of vespers, when my boat, which was ahead of the others, saw a point formed by the land, and on the other side was a very wide river;[15] and I gave orders to drop anchor on a little island formed by the point, to await the other boats. The governor refused to join us; instead he put into a bay very near there in which there were many little islands, and we all gathered there and took fresh water out of the sea, for a strong current of the river entered the sea there. And we went ashore on that island to roast some maize from our supplies, for we had been eating it raw for two days; but as we found no firewood there, we decided to go to the river that was behind the point, a league away; and as we went the current was so strong that we were unable to arrive at all; rather, it carried us away from the land, as we labored and struggled to reach it.

The north wind that came off the shore began to rise so much that it swept us out to sea against our will: and half a league into it, we dropped anchor and found that with thirty fathoms of line we could not find bottom, and we could not decide whether it was the current that made it impossible to take soundings; we sailed like this for two days, still laboring to reach land; and at the end of the two days, a little before sunrise, we saw a great deal of smoke on the coast. And attempting to reach the place, we found ourselves in three fathoms of water, and because it was dark we dared not land, for as we had seen so much smoke we believed that some new danger might come to us without our being able to see, owing to the great darkness, what we ought to do. And so we determined to wait until morning, and when dawn broke each boat was out of sight of the others. I found that I was in thirty fathoms, and continuing on my way, at the hour of vespers I saw two boats, and as I went toward them I saw that the first was the governor's, who asked me what I thought we ought to do. I told him that he must overtake the boat that was sailing ahead of us and not leave it by any means, and that with the three boats together we should continue wherever God led us. He answered that this could not be done, for the boat was far out to sea and he wanted to land; and that if I wished to follow it, I should tell the men in my boat to take the oars and go to work, because we would reach land only by the strength of our arms. A captain who was in his boat, named Pantoja, advised him to do this, telling him that if we did not reach land that day we would not do so in six more, and that during that time we must surely die of hunger.

When I saw what his decision was I took my oar, and so did all the others in my boat who were able to do so, and we rowed until almost sunset; but since the governor's boat carried the healthiest and strongest people among us all, there was no way we could follow him or keep up with it. When I saw this I asked him to give me a line from his boat to help me follow him, and he answered me that if they themselves reached land that night, it was as much as they could do. I told him that in view of the little chance we had to follow him and do what he had ordered, he had better tell me what his orders to me were. He answered that this was no time for some to give orders to others, that each must do what seemed best to him to save his life, and that that was what he intended to do. And so saying, he drew away with his boat, and as I could not follow I caught up with the other boat that was well out to sea, which waited for me; and when I had reached it, I found that it was the boat that carried Captains Peñalosa and Téllez.

And so we sailed on together for four days, eating a ration of a half-handful of raw maize daily. At the end of these four days we were overtaken by a storm that caused us to lose sight of the other boat, and through God's great mercy toward us we did not all founder, so bad was the weather, and with its being winter and very cold and the hunger we had suffered for so many days. As a result of the buffeting we received from the sea, next day the men began to fail very much, so that by sunset all those in my boat were lying heaped upon one another, so near to death that few of them were conscious, and by this time not five men among them were fit to stand. And when night fell only the mate and I were capable of sailing the boat, and two hours after nightfall the mate told me to take over, for he was in such a condition that he thought he would die that night. And so I took the helm, and after midnight I went to see if the mate was dead, and he told me that he was in fact better and that he would steer until morning.

At that moment I would surely have much preferred to accept death than see so many people before my eyes in such a condition. And after the mate took charge of the boat I rested a little, but very restlessly, and nothing was further from my thoughts than sleep. Near dawn I thought I heard breakers, for as the coast was low the waves made a great deal of noise, and called to the mate in alarm; he answered that he thought we were near land, and we made soundings and found a depth of seven fathoms, and he thought we ought to stay at sea until daylight. And so I took an oar and rowed parallel to the land, for we were a league away from it, and then turned our stern to the sea. And when we were near land a wave took us that tossed the boat out of the water a good horseshoe's cast; and with the great jolt it gave, almost all the men in the boat who were half dead came to themselves. And as they saw that land was near, they began to slip over the side and crawl on hands and feet, and as they came ashore where there were some gullies, we made a fire and cooked some maize that we had with us and found some rainwater; and with the heat of the fire the men revived and began to recover their spirits somewhat. The day we arrived there was the sixth of November.

CHAPTER XI

Of What Befell Lope de Oviedo
with Some Indians

After the men had eaten I sent Lope de Oviedo, who was stronger and hardier than anyone else, to go to some trees that were nearby and climb one of them, to find out what sort of country we were in and try to gain some idea of it. He did this and realized that we were on an island[16] and saw that the earth on the mainland was trampled like the ground where livestock have often passed, and this made him think that it was Christian territory, and he told us so. I told him to go and look again more carefully, and to see if there were paths there that could be followed, but not to go too far away because of possible danger. He went and, finding a path, walked along it for about half a league and found some Indian huts that were empty because the Indians had gone out into the countryside; and he took one of their pots and a little dog[17] and a few mullet and came back to us.

And as we thought him long in returning, I sent two other Christians to look for him and find out what had happened to him, and they caught sight of him nearby and saw that three Indians with bows and arrows were following him and calling to him, and he was answering them by signs.

And so he reached the place where we were and the Indians stayed a short distance behind, seated right on the shore; and after half an hour a hundred other Indians armed with arrows came, who whether they were large or not seemed like giants[18] owing to our fear, and they stopped near us, where the first three were. As for us, it was useless to think that anyone could defend himself, for there were scarcely half a dozen who could get up from the ground. The inspector and I went toward them and called to them and they came closer to us; and as best we could we tried to reassure them and ourselves and gave them beads and hawk's bells, and each of them gave me an arrow, which is a sign of friendship; and they told us by signs that they would return in the morning and bring us food, for at the moment they had none.

CHAPTER XII

How the Indians Brought Us Food

Next day as the sun was rising, which was the hour that the Indians had indicated to us, they came to us as they had promised and brought us a large quantity of fish and some roots[19] that they eat and that resemble nuts, some larger and some smaller; most of them are gathered underwater, and with much effort. In the afternoon they returned and brought us more fish and the same roots and had their women and children come to see us, and so they returned rich with the bells and beads that we gave them, and on other days they visited us again with the same things as before. As we saw that we were well supplied with fish and roots and water and the other things that we asked them for, we decided to launch the boats again and continue on our way; and we dug the boat out of the sand in which it was half buried, and we all had to strip and expend a great deal of effort to get it into the water, for we were in such a sorry plight that even much lighter tasks exhausted us. And so, having launched the boat, we were a distance of two crossbow shots[20] into the sea when there came a wave so huge that it soaked us all, and as we were naked and the cold was so great, we let go of the oars, and another wave from the sea overturned the boat. The inspector and two others clung to it to escape death: but quite the opposite happened, for the boat carried them under and they were drowned.

As the coast there is very rugged, the sea in one lurch threw all the others, submerged in the waves and half drowned, onto the shore of the same island, and the only ones missing were the three whom the boat had carried under. The rest of us who escaped were naked as the day we were born and had lost all that we had with us, which though it was not worth much, was everything to us at that time. And since by then it was

November and the cold was very great and we were in such
a plight that one could have counted our bones without difficulty, we looked like the very image of death. Of myself I
can say that I had eaten nothing but roasted maize since the
month of May, and sometimes I had to eat it raw, for though
the horses were slaughtered during the time the boats were
being built, I was never able to eat them and did not eat fish
as many as ten times.

I say this to avoid entering into further explanations, for
anyone can imagine the sorry state we were in. And in addition
to everything I have said, a north wind had started to blow,
so that we were closer to death than to life. But it pleased Our
Lord that, as we searched among the embers of the fire we
had made there, we found fire, with which we made great
bonfires, and thus we were imploring Our Lord for mercy and
pardon for our sins, shedding many tears, each one bewailing
not only his own plight but that of all the others whom he
saw in the same state. And at the hour of sunset the Indians,
believing that we had not left, came looking for us again to
bring us food; but when they saw us in such different circumstances as at first, and in such a strange condition, they were
so frightened that they turned back. I went toward them and
called them and they came, in great consternation; I gave them
to understand by signs how a boat had sunk and three of our
number had drowned, and there before them they saw two
corpses and saw that those of us who were left were on the
way to becoming corpses too. When the Indians saw the disaster that had come upon us and the disaster we were in,
with so much ill luck and misery, they sat down among us
and, with the great grief and pity they felt on seeing us in such
a desperate plight, all of them began to weep loudly, and so
sincerely that they could be heard a long way off, and this
lasted more than half an hour; and certainly, to see that those
uncivilized and savage men, like brutes, were so sorry for us,
caused me and others in our company to feel still more grief
and the full realization of our misfortune.

When this weeping had subsided I questioned the Christians
and said that if they were in agreement I would ask those

Indians to take us to their houses; and some of them, who had been in New Spain, answered that there could be no question of it, for if they took us to their houses they would sacrifice us to their idols. But in view of the fact that there was no other solution, and that if we took any other course death would be closer and more certain, I paid no heed to what they were saying; rather, I implored the Indians to take us to their houses, and they showed great pleasure at the prospect and told us to wait for a little while and they would do as we wished; and then thirty of them loaded themselves with firewood and went to their houses, which were a good distance away; and we stayed with the others until near nightfall, when they seized us, and holding us closely and in great haste, went with us to their houses. And because it was very cold, and fearing that some of us might die or collapse on the way, they provided four or five very large bonfires placed at intervals and warmed us at each one; and as soon as they saw that we had acquired some strength and warmth they took us to the next fire, so quickly that they scarcely allowed our feet to touch the ground, and in this way we went to their houses, where we found that they had built a house for us with many fires in it; and by an hour after the time we arrived they began to dance and make great revelry (which lasted all night), though for us there was neither pleasure nor revelry nor sleep, waiting to know when they were going to sacrifice us; and next morning they again gave us fish and roots and such good treatment that we felt a little safer and lost to some degree our fear of sacrifice.

CHAPTER XIII

How We Had News of Other Christians

On that same day I saw one of those Indians who had barter goods and realized that they were not of the same kind we had given them; and on asking him where they had come from, the Indians replied by signs that other men like us, who were farther inland, had given the goods to them. Upon seeing this I sent two Christians with two Indians to show those people to them, and they discovered them not far away. They too were coming to look for us because the Indians who were there had told them about us; and these were the captains Andrés Dorantes and Alonso del Castillo with all the men from their boat. And when they had reached us they were horrified to see the condition we were in, and exceedingly sorrowful because they had no clothing to give us except what they themselves were wearing. And they stayed there with us and told us how, on the fifth of that same month, their boat had capsized a league and a half from there, and they had escaped without losing anything, and all of us together agreed to repair their boat, and to see that those who had the strength and inclination to do so should sail in it; the others, to stay there until they had recovered their strength and then to travel as best they could along the coast and wait there until God brought them, along with us, to Christian lands.

No sooner had we decided upon this than we set to work. And before we launched the boat Tavera, one of the gentlemen in our company, died; and the boat we had intended to go in foundered and could not float, and later it sank. And as we were in the condition I have described and most of us were naked, and the weather was too severe for marching and crossing rivers and swimming inlets, and as we lacked any provisions at all or any way to carry them, we decided to do what need forced us to, which was to spend the winter there. And we also agreed that four of the strongest men should go to Pánuco, believing it to be nearby; and that if God Our Lord was pleased to bring them there, they would report how we had remained on that island, and our need and hardship. These were very strong swimmers, and one of them was a Portuguese named Alvaro Fernández, a carpenter and seaman; the second was named Méndez and the third Figueroa, a native of Toledo; the fourth, Astudillo, came from Zafra. They took with them an Indian who was a native of the island.

CHAPTER XIV

How Four Christians Departed

A few days after these four Spaniards had departed there came a time of cold and storms so severe that the Indians could not gather their roots and could make no use at all of the creeks where they fished; and as the houses were so flimsy the people began to die, and five Christians who were encamped on the beach came to such straits that they ate one another until only one was left, who survived because there was no one left to eat him. The names of these men were as follows: Sierra, Diego López, Corral, Palacios, and Gonzalo Ruiz. The Indians were so indignant about this, and there was so much outrage among them, that undoubtedly if they had seen this when it began to happen they would have killed the men, and all of us would have been in dire peril; in a word, within a very short time only fifteen of the eighty men[21] from both parties who had reached the island were left alive; and after the death of these men, a stomach ailment afflicted the Indians of the land from which half of them died, and they believed that it was we who were killing them; and as they were wholly convinced of this, they agreed among themselves to kill those of us who were left.

When they were on the point of carrying this out, an Indian who was holding me told them not to believe that it was we who were killing them, for if we had had such power so many of our own would not have died, as they had seen, without our being able to prevent it, and that now there were very few of us left, and none of us was doing any harm or injury; that it was best to leave us alone. And it was Our Lord's will that the others followed his advice and opinion, and thus their plan was thwarted. We gave to this island the name of Malhado, Isle of Ill Fortune. The folk that we found there are tall and handsome; they have no other arms than bows and arrows,

46

in the use of which they are extremely skillful. The men have one nipple pierced from side to side, and some of them have both, and they wear a reed two and one-half handbreadths long and two fingers thick stuck through the hole; they also have their lower lip pierced, and a piece of reed as slender as half a finger stuck through it.

The women are the ones who do the hard work. They live on this island from October to the end of February. Their staple food is the roots I have mentioned, gathered underwater in November and December. They have creeks and have no more fish at this time; from then on they eat roots. At the end of February they go elsewhere to seek food, for then the roots begin to sprout and are no longer good. Of all people on earth they are the ones who love their children most and give them the best treatment; and when it happens that someone loses a child, the parents and kinfolk and the whole tribe weep for him, and their lamentation lasts for a whole year, for every morning before dawn the parents begin to weep first of all and after them the whole tribe, and they do the same at dawn and at midday; and after they have bewailed them for a year they do funeral honors to the dead child and wash and clean off the soot with which they have covered their bodies.

They mourn for all their dead in this way, except for the old, of whom they take no heed, for they say that they have had their time and are of no use to anyone; rather, they occupy space and take food from the children's mouths. Their custom is to bury the dead, except for those among them who are medicine men; these they burn, and while the fire is burning they all dance and make great revelry, and they make powder out of the bones. And after a year has passed, when they perform the funeral honors, all of them scarify themselves and give that powder made of the bones to the kinfolk to drink, dissolved in water. Each man has a recognized wife. The medicine men are the freest among them: they can have two or three wives, and there is great friendship and harmony among the wives. When it chances that someone marries off his daughter, beginning on that day the wife carries to her father's house everything that the man who has taken her to wife has killed by hunting or fishing, and he dares not touch or eat any of it; and they bring him food from his father-in-law's house. And in all this time neither the father-in-law nor the mother-in-law enters his house, nor does he enter the house of his parents-in-law, nor that of his brothers-in-law, and if by chance they encounter each other in any place, they move a crossbow shot's distance away from each other; and while they are drawing apart from one another they carry their heads low and keep their eyes on the ground, for they hold it a bad thing to see or speak to each other.

The women are free to communicate and converse with their parents-in-law and kinfolk. And this custom is adhered to from the island to more than fifty leagues inland. There is another custom, and it is that when a son or brother dies those who live in the house where he died do not seek food for three months; rather than do so they would die of hunger, and their kinfolk and neighbors bring them what they need to eat. And since during the time we were there so many of their people died, there was great hunger in most of their houses because they also respected this custom and ceremony; and those who did search for food, no matter how great their effort, could find but little because of the severe weather. And for this reason the Indians who were holding me left the island and went to the mainland in canoes, to some bays where there were many oysters; and for three months of the year they eat nothing else and drink very bad water. There is great scarcity of firewood, and great abundance of mosquitoes. Their houses are built of reed mats on a foundation of many oyster shells, and they sleep naked on top of these shells if they are lucky enough to have any. And we were in this situation until the end of April, when we went to the seacoast, where we ate blackberries for the entire month, during which the Indians did not cease to hold their rites and festivals.

CHAPTER XV

What Befell Us in the Isle of Ill Fortune

On that island that I have described they tried to make us into medicine men, without examining us or asking for credentials, for they cure illnesses by blowing on the sick person, and by blowing and using their hands they cast the illness out of him; and they ordered us to do the same and to be of some use. We laughed at it, saying that it was a joke and that we did not know how to heal, and because of this they withheld our food until we did as they had told us. And seeing our resistance, one Indian told me that I did not know what I was talking about when I said that what he knew would be of no use to me, for stones and other things that grow in the fields have virtue, and by using a hot stone and passing it over the stomach he could cure and take away pain; and we, who were superior men, surely had even greater virtue and power. At last we were under such pressure that we had to do it, without fear that we would be held up to scorn for it. The manner they have of curing is as follows: when they find that they are ill they call for a doctor, and after they are cured they not only give him everything they possess but search among their kinfolk for things to give him.

What the doctor does is make some cuts in the place where the patient has the pain and suck all around them. They perform cautery by fire, a thing that is held among them to be very beneficial, and I have tried this and had good results with it; and then they blow on the place where the pain is, and with this they believe that the illness is cured. The way in which we cured was by making the sign of the cross over them and blowing on them and reciting a Pater Noster and an Ave Maria; and then we prayed as best we could to God Our Lord to give them health and inspire them to give us good treatment. God

Our Lord, and His mercy, willed that as soon as we made the sign of the cross over them, all those for whom we prayed told the others that they were well and healthy; and because of this they gave us good treatment and went without food themselves in order to give it to us and gave us hides and other small things. The hunger that we endured there was so great that I often spent three days without eating anything at all, and they also were hungry; and it seemed impossible to me that I could go on living, though later I found myself in even greater hunger and need, as I will recount below.

The Indians who were holding Alonso del Castillo and Andrés Dorantes and the others who were left alive, as they were of a different language and different family, crossed over to another part of the mainland to eat oysters and stayed there until the first day of April; and then they returned to the island, which was about two leagues from the mainland where the water was widest, and the island was half a league wide and five leagues long. All the people of this land go about naked; only the women cover part of their bodies with a sort of wool that grows on trees.[22] Young girls cover themselves with deerskins. They are a very generous people, sharing whatever they own with others. There is no chief among them. All those of one family stay together. In that land there are two kinds of language: some Indians they call Capoques, and the others Han; it is their custom, when two persons meet and see each other from time to time, to spend half an hour weeping before they speak; and after they have done this the person who is being visited stands up first and gives the other everything that he possesses; and the other receives it and a little later goes off with it, and even sometimes, after he has received it, both go away without speaking a word. They have other strange customs, but I have related the chief and most important ones, in order to continue and recount the rest of the things that befell us.

CHAPTER XVI

How the Christians Departed from the Isle of Ill Fortune

After Dorantes and Castillo returned to the island they gathered all the Christians together, for they were somewhat scattered, and there were fourteen of them in all. As I have said, I was on the other side, on the mainland, where my Indians had taken me and where I had been so gravely ill that, if any other thing had given me some hope of life, the illness would have been enough to make me wholly lose it. And as the Christians learned of this, they gave one of the Indians the sable cloak that we had taken from the chief, as we mentioned above, to carry them over to the place where I was, to see me. And twelve came, for two of them were so weak that they dared not bring them along. The names of those who came at that time were: Alonso del Castillo, Andrés Dorantes and Diego Dorantes; Valdivieso, Estrada, Tostado, Chaves, Gutiérrez, Asturiano (a priest), Diego de Huelva, Estebanico the black, and Benítez. And when they had reached the mainland they found another of our number named Francisco de León, and all thirteen of them were living along the coast. And as soon as they had crossed over, the Indians who were holding me told me of it, and that Jerónimo de Alaniz and Lope de Oviedo had stayed on the island. My illness prevented me from following them, nor did I see them.

I was obliged to stay with these same Indians of the island for more than a year, and because of the hard labor they assigned me and the bad treatment they gave me, I decided to escape from them and go to the Indians who live in the woods and on the mainland, who are called Chorrucos,[23] for I could not bear the life I was leading with these others; for among many other labors, I had to gather the roots they used for food, under water and among the reeds where they grew on the land; and my fingers were so lacerated from this that if a blade of straw touched them they bled, and the reeds tore me all over my body because many reeds were broken and I had to go into the middle of them with the little clothing that I wore, as I have said. And so I carried out my plan of going over to the other Indians and was somewhat better off with them; and because I became a trader I tried to take advantage of this trade as best I knew how, and hence they fed me and gave me good treatment and enjoined me to go from one place to another for things that they needed, because owing to the constant state of war among them there was not much traveling or trading. And, with my tradings and merchandise, I could go into the interior of the country as much as I liked and would travel up and down the coast for a distance of forty or fifty leagues. The larger part of my trading was in pieces of sea snails, and their hearts, and shells that the Indians use to cut a fruit resembling beans, which they use as medicine and in their dances and festivals, and this is the most highly prized thing among them; and sea beads, and other things. So this was what I carried on my journeys inland.[24]

And in exchange and trade for this I brought hides and the ocher that they use to smear on themselves and dye their faces and hair; flints for arrowheads, glue and dried reeds to make them with, and tassels that are made of deer hair dyed red; and this trade suited me very well, for by traveling in the course of it I was free to go wherever I wished and was not obliged to do anything and was not a slave; and everywhere I went they gave me good treatment and food on account of my merchandise. And the most important part of it was that, as I traveled about this business, I was seeking how to go forward, and I was very well known among the Indians; they rejoiced greatly when they saw me and when I brought them things that they needed, and those who did not know me tried to see me and wanted to see me, because of my fame among them. The hardships I endured during this time would be long in the telling, danger and hunger as well as cold and storms, many of which overtook me out in the countryside and alone, from which I escaped by the great mercy of God Our Lord. And for this reason I did not exercise my trade in winter, for it was a time when they themselves, shut into their huts and camps, could do nothing for themselves or protect themselves. The time that I spent in this land was almost six years,[25] alone among them and as naked as they. The reason that I stayed so long was that I wished to take with me a Christian named Lope de Oviedo. His other companion, Alaniz, who had stayed with him when Alonso del Castillo and Andrés Dorantes departed with all the others, had died soon after, and in order to take Oviedo away from there I went over to the island every year and implored him to go with me, as best we could, to seek other Christians; and every year he held me back, saying that we would go next year. In short, at last I got him out of there and helped him cross the inlet and the four rivers that are on the coast, for he did not know how to swim. And so we went forward with a few Indians until we reached an arm of the sea that is a league wide and deep everywhere, and to judge from what we thought and saw, it is the one called Holy Spirit;[26] and on the other side of it we saw some Indians who had come to see ours, and they told us that farther on there were three men like us, and the Indians told us their names.

And when we asked about the others, they replied that all of them had died of cold and hunger. And that those very Indians who lived farther on had killed Diego Dorantes and Valdivieso and Diego de Huelva for their own amusement, because they had moved from one house to another; and that the other Indians who were neighbors of theirs, with whom Captain Dorantes was at present, had killed Esquivel and Méndez because of a dream they had had. We asked them about the condition of the survivors: they told us that they were very ill treated, for the youths and other Indians, who among those folk are very lazy and cruel, often kicked and struck and beat them, and that was the kind of life they were leading.

We tried to find out what the land was like farther on, and what supplies of food there might be in it; they replied that it was very sparsely populated and that there was nothing in it to eat, and that they were dying of cold because they had no hides or anything else to cover themselves. They also said that if we wished to see those three Christians, the Indians who were holding them would come two days later to eat nuts[27] in a place one league's distance away, on the bank of that river; and to demonstrate that what they had told us of the ill treatment of the others was true, while we were with them they struck and beat my companion, nor did I escape either, for they threw many lumps of mud at us, and each day they held arrows over our hearts, telling us that they wanted to kill us as they had our other comrades. And my companion Lope de Oviedo, fearing this, said that he wanted to return with some women of that tribe with whom we had crossed the inlet some distance back. I entreated him not to do so and made many efforts, but in no way could I dissuade him, and so he returned and I remained alone with those Indians, who are called Queuenes; and the others, with whom he went, are called Deaguanes.

CHAPTER XVII

How the Indians Came
and Brought Andrés Dorantes and
Castillo and Estebanico

Two days after Lope de Oviedo had departed, the Indians who were holding Alonso del Castillo and Andrés Dorantes came to the same place they had told us of, to gather those nuts that they grind together with grains to feed themselves for two months of the year, eating nothing else; and they do not even do this every year, for they come in alternate years; the nuts are the size of those in Galicia, and the trees are very large and there are a great number of them. An Indian told me that the Christians had arrived, and that if I wished to see them I must slip away and escape to a part of a wood that he pointed out to me; for he and other kinfolk of his were going to see those Indians, and that they would take me with them to where the Christians were. I trusted them and determined to do it, for they had a language different from that of my Indians. And having done it, next day they came and found me in the place they had indicated, and so they took me with them.

When I came near the place where they were camped Andrés Dorantes came out to see who it was, for the Indians had also told him that a Christian was coming; and when he saw me he was very astonished, for they had thought me dead for many a day, and the Indians had told him so. We gave many thanks to God because we were together, and that day was one of the happiest we had had in our lives. And when we came to the place where Castillo was, they asked me where I was going. I told them that my plan was to cross over into Christian lands, and that I was going to follow that trail in search of them. Andrés Dorantes answered that for many days he had been imploring Castillo and Estebanico to go forward, and that they dared not do it because they did not know how to swim and greatly feared the rivers and inlets that they would have to cross, for there are many in that land. And because God Our Lord had been pleased to save me among so many trials and illnesses and had brought me at last into their company, they decided to escape, and I agreed to help them cross the rivers and inlets that we might encounter; and they assured me that they would in no way let the Indians know about me or that I wanted to go on, for then they would kill me; and therefore it was necessary for me to stay with them for six months, which was the season when those Indians went to another part of the country to eat the fruit of the prickly pear.[28]

This is a fruit of the size of an egg, and it is red and black and has a very good taste. For three months of the year they eat the fruit and nothing else, for during the time that they are picking it other Indians from farther inland come to see them, bringing bows, to trade and exchange with them; and when those Indians came back we would flee from ours and return with the others. Under this agreement I stayed there, and they gave me as a slave to an Indian who was with Dorantes, who was one-eyed, as were his wife and son and another Indian who was with him: so that all of them had only one eye each. These Indians are called Mareames, and Castillo was with others, neighbors of theirs, called Yguazes. And while I was there the other Christians told me that after they had left the Isle of Ill Fortune they had found overturned on the shore the boat that had carried the auditor and the friars; and that as they crossed those rivers, which are four, very large and with swift currents, the boats in which they were crossing were carried out to sea, where four of them were drowned, and so they went on until they crossed the inlet and did so with great difficulty, and fifteen leagues farther on they found another; and by the time they arrived there two comrades had already died during the sixty leagues they had covered, and all the rest of them were on the point of death, and during the whole journey they had eaten nothing but crabs and a kind of kelp.

And they said that when they reached this last inlet, they found Indians there who were eating blackberries, and when they saw the Christians they left there and went to another point of land, and that while they tried and sought a way to cross the inlet, an Indian and a Christian crossed over to them; and that when he arrived they recognized Figueroa, one of the four whom we had sent ahead on the Isle of Ill Fortune; and he told them how he and his comrades had reached that place, where two of them and an Indian had died, all of them from cold and hunger, for they had arrived and stayed there under the most severe weather conditions in the world; and that he and Méndez had been captured by the Indians. And that while they were with them Méndez had escaped, traveling to the best of his knowledge in the direction of Pánuco, and that the Indians had gone after him and killed him; and that while he was with these Indians he learned from them that there was a Christian with the Mareames who had crossed over to the other side, and he had found him with the tribe that they call Queuenes; and that this Christian was Hernando de Esquivel, a native of Badajoz, who had come in company with the commissary, and that he learned from Esquivel the fate of the governor and the auditor and the others; he told him that the auditor and the friars had beached their boat between the rivers, and as they journeyed along the coast the governor's boat came to land with his people, and he sailed with his boat until they came to that large inlet, and that he returned there to take the men and crossed them over to the other side and returned for the auditor and the friars and all the others.

And Esquivel told how, when they had disembarked, the governor revoked the authority that the auditor had had as his lieutenant and gave the office to a captain whom he had brought with him, whose name was Pantoja; and that the governor stayed in his boat and refused to go ashore that night, and a mate and a page, who was ill, stayed with him; and they had no water in the boat or anything to eat, and in the middle of the night the north wind began to blow so fiercely that it took the boat out to sea without anyone seeing it go, for they had no anchor but a stone. And that they never learned anything more of him, and that in view of this, the men who were left on land continued along the coast and, as they were so much hindered by the water they had to cross, made rafts with great difficulty, in which they crossed to the other side; and as they pursued their march they reached a wooded point of land on the edge of the water and found Indians who, when they saw them coming, loaded their dwellings into their canoes and crossed over to the coast on the other side; the Christians, considering the time of year, for this was in November, stayed in those woods because they found water and firewood and some few crabs and shellfish, but little by little they began to die of cold and hunger there.

In addition to this Pantoja, who had become lieutenant, treated them very badly; and Sotomayor, the brother of Vasco Porcallo, from the island of Cuba, who had come in the fleet as an officer of high rank, was unable to bear it. He rebelled against him and gave him such a blow that Pantoja died of it; and so they gradually died off. And the others dried the flesh of the ones who died, and the last to die was Sotomayor; and Esquivel dried his flesh and, by eating it, survived until the first day of March, when an Indian among those who had fled came to see if they were dead and took Esquivel with him, and while he was a captive of this Indian Figueroa spoke with him and learned from him everything that had happened and implored him to accompany him so that both could travel in the direction of Pánuco; Esquivel refused to do this, saying that he had learned from the friars that Pánuco was behind them, and so he stayed there and Figueroa went to the coast, where he spent most of his time.

CHAPTER XVIII

Of the Report Given to Figueroa
by Esquivel

Figueroa told this whole story according to the account that Esquivel had given him, and it passed from hand to hand and reached me, and thus is the means by which the end of all that fleet can be seen and known, and the particular things that happened to each man.[29] And he said still more: that if the Christians stayed in the vicinity for some time, it was possible that they might see Esquivel, for they knew that he had escaped from that Indian he was with to another tribe called the Mareames, who were neighbors of theirs. And as I have just said, he and the Asturian would have liked to go over to other Indians who were farther on, but because the Indians who were holding them heard of it, they attacked them and beat them often, and stripped the Asturian naked and pierced his arm with an arrow; and at last they escaped by running away, and the Christians stayed with those Indians and arranged with them to be accepted as their slaves, even though while they were serving them the Christians were maltreated by them as never man nor slave had been before; for of the six that they held captive, not content with striking them frequently and beating them and pulling out their beards to amuse themselves, they killed three of them merely because they moved from one house to another; and those three were the ones whom I listed above: Diego Dorantes and Valdivieso and Diego de Huelva.

And the remaining three expected to end in the same way; and rather than endure this life, Andrés Dorantes ran away and went over to the Mareames, who were the Indians with whom Esquivel had gone; and they told him how they had

held Esquivel there and how, while he was there, he had tried
to run away because a woman had dreamed that he was going
to kill her child; and the Indians went after him and killed him
and showed Andrés Dorantes his sword and his beads and
book[30] and other belongings of his. These Indians do this because of a custom of theirs, and it is that they kill even their
own children as a result of dreams, and when daughters are
born to them they let the dogs eat them and throw them away.
The reason they do this, according to them, is that all the
Indians in that land are their enemies and they carry on con-
tinual warfare with them; and if by any chance their enemies
should marry their daughters, these enemies would increase
so much that they would conquer them and take them as
slaves; and for this reason they preferred to kill their daughters
rather than let a possible enemy be born to them.

We asked them, why did they not marry with themselves
and also among themselves? They said that to marry women
to their kinfolk was a bad thing, and that it was much better
to kill them than to give them to their own kin or to their
enemies; and both they and their neighbors called the Yguazes
have this custom, but only they, for none of the other tribes
in the land practice it. And when these Indians want to marry
they buy wives from their enemies, and the price each man
gives for his wife is a bow, the best that can be procured, with
two arrows, and if perchance he does not own a bow, a fishing
net two cubits wide and one long; they kill their own children
and trade in those of others; their marriages last only as long
as they are happy together, and they dissolve marriages by the
use of an amulet. Dorantes was with these Indians, and after
a few days he escaped. Castillo and Estebanico came over to
the mainland to the Yguazes.[31]

All these people are users of arrows and are well built,
though not as tall as those we left behind; and they pierce one
nipple and their lips. Their principal food is roots of two or
three different kinds, and they search for them throughout the
land; the roots are very bad to eat and swell the bellies of those
who eat them. It takes two days to roast them, and many of
the roots are extremely bitter; in addition to this, gathering

them is very hard work. These people suffer so much from hunger that they cannot do without the roots and will wander for two or three leagues in search of them. Occasionally they kill deer and at times catch a fish or two; but this is so little and their hunger so great that they eat spiders and ants' eggs and worms and lizards and salamanders and snakes, and vipers such as kill the men that they bite; and they eat earth and wood and everything they can lay their hands on, and dung of deer and other things I will not mention; and I firmly believe that if there were stones in that land they would eat them. They keep the bones of the fish that they eat, and those of snakes and other things, to grind them all together later and eat the powder of them. Among these Indians the men do not encumber themselves or carry anything of weight; but women and the old carry heavy things, for they are the folk that these Indians consider least.

They do not love their children as much as those we described before. There are some among them who practice the sin against nature. The women are worked very hard and long, for in the twenty-four hours they have only six hours of rest between day and night, and spend most of the night tending their ovens to dry those roots that they eat. And as soon as day dawns they begin to dig and carry firewood and water to their houses and put in order the things that they need. Most of these Indians are great thieves, for though they get on well among themselves, if one so much as turns his head, even his son or his father will rob him of whatever he can. They are tremendous liars and great drunkards and drink a certain kind of drink for this purpose.[32] They are so accustomed to running that, without rest and without tiring, they can run from morning to night and run down a deer, and they kill many in this way, for they pursue them until they are tired and sometimes capture them alive. Their houses are made of mats laid upon four arches; they carry these mats on their backs and move every two or three days in search of food; they sow nothing that they can make use of; they are a very cheerful people no matter how hungry they may be, and this is why they never cease to hold their festivals and dances.[33]

The best season of the year for them is when they eat the fruits of the prickly pear, for then they are not hungry and spend all their time in dancing, and they eat the fruits day and night as long as they last; they squeeze them and open them and set them to dry and after they are dry put them in bags, like figs, and keep them to eat on the road, and they grind the skins and make a powder of them. Many times when we were with these people we went hungry for three or four days, for there was nothing to eat; and to cheer us they would tell us not to be sad, that soon there would be prickly pears, and that we would eat many of them and drink their juice, and would have big bellies and be very content and happy and feel no hunger at all. And from the time that they told us this until the prickly pears were ready to eat was a span of five or six months; and so we had to wait those six months, and when it was time we went to eat them. In that land we encountered a very large number of mosquitoes of three different kinds, which are very bad and annoying, and during all the rest of the summer they gave us great trouble. And to defend ourselves against them we would build many fires around the people, of rotten and wet wood so that the fire would not burn and would emit a great deal of smoke; and this defense gave us another sort of trouble, for we did nothing but weep all night long because of the smoke that got into our eyes, and in addition to this there was the heat that those many fires caused; and we would go to sleep along the coast, and if we occasionally managed to fall asleep they would remind us with beatings to go back and tend the fires.

The Indians who live inland have another practice that is even more intolerable than the one I have described, and it is to run with firebrands in their hands, burning the woods and fields that they encounter, both to drive away the mosquitoes and to force lizards and other similar things out of the ground, to eat them. And they kill deer, too, by surrounding them with many fires. And they also do this to deprive the animals of grazing places, for then their need causes them to go where the Indians want them to go, and the Indians never set up their houses except in places that have water and firewood.

Sometimes they carry all these supplies and go in search of deer, which ordinarily are in places that have no water or wood; and on the day they arrive they kill deer and whatever other things they can and squander all the water and wood in cooking and in the fires they make to defend themselves against the mosquitoes, and then they wait another day to gather something to carry on the road. And when they leave, they are so bitten by mosquitoes that you would think they had the disease of Saint Lazarus the Leper. In this way they satisfy their hunger two or three times a year, at the cost of the great efforts I have described; and because I have passed through it I can avouch that no hardship in the world is its equal. There are many deer in the land and other birds and animals of the kind I have described earlier.

They hunt a sort of cattle there, and I have seen them three times and eaten them, and I think that they are about the size of those in Spain; they have small, puny horns and very long hair, woolly like woollen cloth; some are dark brown in color and others are black, and in my opinion they have better and heavier meat than Spanish cattle.[34] From the smaller animals the Indians make cloaks to cover themselves, and from the larger beasts they make shoes and shields; these animals come from the north and travel through the land as far as the coast of Florida and range over the landscape for more than four hundred leagues, and in all this distance through the valleys in which they come, the people that live there come down upon them and live off them and distribute large quantities of their hides throughout the land.

CHAPTER XIX

How the Indians Separated Us

At the end of the six months that I had agreed upon with the Christians, waiting to carry out the plan we had made,[35] the Indians went to gather prickly pears, in a place some thirty leagues from the place where they were; and when we were about to make our escape, the Indians we were with quarreled with one another over a woman and struck and beat and injured one another; and because they were so angry, each one took his house and went his way, whence it was necessary that we Christians who were there also had to separate, and there was no way we could meet again until the next year. And during this time I led a very hard life, as much by reason of great hunger as of the bad treatment I received from the Indians, which was such that I tried three times to escape from my masters, and all of them went looking for me and did their best to kill me. And God Our Lord in His mercy deigned to keep and protect me from them. And when the season of prickly pears came again, we were reunited in that same place.

On the very same day that we had agreed to escape and had named the day, the Indians separated us and each one went his way, and I said to my other comrades that I would wait for them in the place where the prickly pears were until the moon was full, and that day was the first of September and the first day of the moon; and I warned them that if in this period of time they did not come as agreed, I would go alone and leave them behind.

And so we separated and each one went with his Indians, and I was with mine until the thirteenth day of the moon; and I had it in mind to escape to other Indians when the moon was full. And on the thirteenth day of the month Andrés Dorantes and Estebanico came to where I was and told me how they had left Castillo with other Indians called Anagados, and that they were camped near there, and that they had suffered many hardships and had been lost. And that on the following day our Indians would move camp closer to where Castillo was, and they were going to join with the Indians who held him and make friends with them, for up to that time they had been at war; and in this way we recovered Castillo. During the whole time we were eating the prickly pears we were thirsty, and to relieve this we drank their juice and squeezed it into a hollow that we made in the ground, and when it was full we drank to our hearts' content. The juice is sweet and the color of syrup; the Indians do this because they have no other vessels. There are many kinds of prickly pears and some among them are very good, though all of them seemed good to me and hunger never gave me a chance to choose among them or to give the least consideration to which were best.

Almost all of these people drink rainwater, gathered in different places, for although there are rivers, since they never stay in one place they never possess known and recognized sources of water. Throughout the land are large and beautiful pastures and very good grazing for livestock, and it seems to me that it would be a very fruitful land if it were cultivated and peopled by civilized folk. We saw no mountains in any part of it during the time that we were there. Those Indians told us that farther on were others, called Camoles,[36] who lived near the coast and had killed all the men who came in the boat with Peñalosa and Téllez, and that they had reached shore so weak that they did not defend themselves even from being killed, and so the Indians slaughtered all of them; and they showed us clothing and weapons of theirs and said that the boat was beached there. This was the fifth boat that was missing, for we have told already how the governor's boat was carried out to sea, and they had seen that of the auditor and the friars cast up and overturned on the shore, and Esquivel told us of their end. The two boats that held Castillo and Dorantes and me, as we have recounted, sank off the Isle of Ill Fortune.

CHAPTER XX

How We Escaped

Two days after we had made the move, we commended ourselves to God Our Lord and made our escape, trusting in the
fact that though it was late in the season and the prickly pears
were almost gone, we could travel a fair distance with the fruit
that was left in the countryside. As we traveled that day, in
considerable fear that the Indians would follow us, we saw
some smoke and, toward the end of the day, reached it, where
we espied an Indian who, when he saw us coming toward him,
fled without waiting for our arrival; we sent the black after
him, and when the Indian saw that he was alone, he waited
for him. The black told him that we were looking for the people
who were making that smoke. He replied that their houses
were near there and that he would guide us to them: and so
we followed him and he ran to tell the people that we were
coming, and at sunset we saw the houses, and at a distance
of a couple of crossbow shots before we reached them we found
four Indians who were waiting for us and received us kindly.
We told them in the Mareame language that we were looking
for them, and they indicated that they were happy to have our
company; and so they took us to their houses and lodged
Dorantes and the black in the house of one medicine man, and
Castillo and me in that of another.

These Indians speak a different language and are called
Avavares[37] and are the ones who were accustomed to bring
bows to our Indians and trade with them, and though they are
of another language and tribe they understand the language
of the Indians we had been with before; and they had arrived
there with their houses on that very day. Then the people
offered us many prickly pears, for they had heard of us, and
how we cured folk, and the marvels that Our Lord did by our

hands. Had we done no more works than these, they were great enough to smooth our way through such sparsely settled territory, and to furnish us with people in a place where often there were none, and to deliver us from so many perils and not allow them to kill us, and to keep us alive through so much hunger, and to incline the hearts of those people to treat us well, as I shall recount.

CHAPTER XXI

How We Cured Some Sufferers There

On the same night that we arrived, some Indians came to Castillo and told him that they had dreadful pains in their heads, imploring him to cure them; and after he had signed them with the cross and commended them to God, the Indians said that all the pains had left them at that very moment; and they went to their houses and brought many prickly pears and a piece of venison, which was something that we could not identify; and as the matter became known among them, many other sick folk came that night to have him cure them, and each one brought a piece of venison, and there were so many of them that we did not know where to put the meat. We offered many thanks to God because His mercy and favors toward us increased daily. And after the cures had been accomplished they began to dance and make their revels and festivals until dawn of the following day; and because of our arrival the festivities lasted for three days, and at the end of them we inquired about the land ahead of us and the people we would find in it, and the supplies of food that were there.

They answered us that throughout that land were many prickly pears, but that the season for them was over, and that no people were there because all had gone to their homes after gathering the prickly pears, and that the land was very cold and few hides were to be found in it. And in view of this, for winter and cold weather were already upon us, we decided to spend the winter with them. Five days after we arrived they set off to look for more prickly pears in a place where there were people of other tribes and languages. And after journeying for five days with very great hunger, for on the way there were no prickly pears or any other kind of fruit, we reached a river where we set up our houses, and when they had been erected we went to find the fruit of some trees of a leguminous kind; and as there are no paths in this part of the country I was slower in finding the place, and the people returned and I was left alone. As I went looking for them that night I became lost, and it pleased God that I found a tree burning and survived the cold of that night by its fire; and in the morning I loaded myself with wood and took two firebrands and again searched for them and traveled in this manner for five days, always with my fire and load of firewood; for if the fire were to go out in a place where there was no wood (and in many places there was none), I would have something with which to make new firebrands and would not be left without a fire, for I had no other protection against the cold, being naked as the day I was born.

And during the nights I had this stratagem: I would go to the thickets of woods near the rivers[38] and stop in them before the sun set, and I would make a hole in the ground and throw into it a quantity of branches, which grew on many trees that were there, and in large quantities; and I would gather together a great deal of firewood that had fallen from the trees and was dry, and around that hole I would make four fires in the shape of a cross. I took care to rebuild the fire at intervals and made bundles of a long sort of straw that grows there, with which I covered myself in the hole and in this way sheltered myself from the nights' cold; and one night some fire fell on the straw with which I was covered, and as I was sleeping in the hole it began to burn very fiercely, and for all my haste in escaping, I was left with singed hair as a mark of the danger I had been in.

During all this time I had not a bite to eat, nor did I find anything that could be eaten; and as my feet were bare the blood ran from them freely. And God had mercy on me, for during all this time there was no wind from the north, for otherwise there was no way in which I could have survived. And after five days I reached the banks of a river where I found my Indians, and they and the Christians had given me up for dead and believed that some viper had bitten me. All were very happy to see me, chiefly the Christians, and they told me that they had journeyed to this place suffering great hunger, and this was the reason they had not searched for me, and that night they gave me some of the prickly pears they had with them. And next day we left there and went to a place where we found many prickly pears, with which we all satisfied our great hunger. And we gave many thanks to Our Lord, for He never withheld His aid from us.

CHAPTER XXII

How They Brought Us More Sick Folk Next Day

Next morning many Indians came there and brought five sick men who were crippled and very ill, and they came looking for Castillo to cure them, and each of the sick men offered his bow and arrows, and he took them, and at sunset made the sign of the cross over them and prayed to God our Lord, and all of us implored Him as best we could to give them health, for He could see that there was no other recourse but to have those people help us and for us to escape from so miserable a life; and He did so with such great mercy that when morning came all of them awoke well and healthy and went away as strong as if they had never had any sickness. This caused very great astonishment among the Indians and inspired us to give many thanks to Our Lord, that we might more fully know His goodness and have the firm hope that He would free us and bring us to where we might serve Him. For myself, I can say that I always had faith in His mercy, that He would surely release me from that captivity, and I always told my comrades so.

When the Indians had departed and taken their healthy Indians with them, we left for a place where others were eating prickly pears, and these others are called Cutalchiches and Maliacones, which are different languages, and with them were some others called Coayos and Susolas, and others from another place called Atayos, and these last were at war with the Susolas, with whom they exchanged arrows every day. And as throughout the land the people spoke of nothing but the mysteries that God Our Lord had performed through us, they came from many places to find us and have us cure them, and two days after they arrived some Indians of the Susola tribe came to us and begged Castillo to go and heal a wounded man and others who were ill, and said that one among them was on the point of death. Castillo was very fearful of his medical powers, especially when the cures were hazardous and dangerous; he believed that his sins would prevent him from successfully curing every case.

The Indians told me that I should go and heal them, for they loved me and remembered that I had cured them during the time of nut gathering and that they had given us nuts and hides in return, and this had happened when I came to join the other Christians; and so I had to go with them, and Dorantes and Estebanico went with me. And when I came near to their settlements I saw the sick man whom we were going to heal, who was dead, for many people were around him weeping and his house had been pulled down, which is a sign that its owner has died. And so when I got there I found the Indian with his eyes rolled up and without any pulse and with all the signs of being dead, as it seemed to me, and Dorantes said the same. I took off a reed mat with which he was covered, and as best I could implored Our Lord to be pleased to give health to that man and all others who had need of it.

And after I had made the sign of the cross and blown on him many times, they brought me his bow and gave it to me, and a bag of crushed prickly pears, and took me to heal many others who were lying in a stupor, and they gave me two more bags of prickly pears that I gave to the Indians who had come with me; and when we had done this we returned to our quarters, and our Indians, the ones to whom I had given the prickly pears, stayed there. And that night they returned to their homes and said that the man who was dead and whom I had healed had stood up in their presence entirely well and had walked and eaten and spoken with them, and that all those whom I had cured were healthy and very happy. This caused great astonishment and consternation, and in all the land no one talked of anything else.[39] All those who heard this news came to look for us, to have us heal them and sign their children with the cross. And when the Indians who were in company with ours, who were the Cutalchiches, had to leave and go to their land, they came to us before they departed and offered us all the prickly pears they had prepared for the journey, without leaving any for themselves, and gave us flintstones as long as a handbreadth and a half, which they use for cutting things and esteem greatly.

They implored us to remember them, and to pray to God that they might always be well, and we promised them this; and so they departed the happiest men in the world, having given us the best they had. We stayed with those Avavares Indians for eight months and reckoned this period by the moon. During all this time the Indians came from many places to seek us and said that we were truly children of the sun. Up to this time Dorantes and the black had not done any healing; but because of the many entreaties we received, coming from many different places to look for us, all of us became medicine men, though I was paramount among us in daring and in attempting any sort of cure.[40] And we never healed anyone who did not then tell us that he was well, and they were so confident that they would be cured if we healed them, that they believed that as long as we were there none of them would have to die.

These and other Indians who lived farther inland told me a very strange thing, and from the reckoning they gave us it seemed that it had happened some fifteen or sixteen years before. They told us that there was in that land a man whom they call Bad Thing,[41] and that he was small of stature and had a beard, though they could never see his face clearly; and that when he came to the house where they were their hair stood on end and they trembled; and then a firebrand, burning, appeared at the door of the house, and then that man entered and took whatever he wanted from them and gave them three great slashes in the side with a very sharp flint a handbreadth wide and two long, and that he put his hand into those slashes and pulled out their entrails, and that he cut off a piece of intestine a handbreadth wide, more or less, and threw it into the fire; and then he would cut them three times on the arm, the second cut being at the elbow, and then he would dislocate it; and soon after that he would set the arm in its place again and lay his hands on the wounds; and they told us that they would then be healed, and that often when they were dancing he appeared among them, sometimes dressed as a woman and at other times as a man, and that when he wished he could take a hut or house and lift it into the air and then, a little later, let it fall with a great crash.

They also told us that often they offered him food and that he never ate, and that they asked him where he came from and where his home was, and he showed them a crack in the earth and said that his house was there below. We laughed very much at these things they told us, making fun of them, and as they saw that we did not believe them they brought many of the people whom they said he had taken; and we saw the knife scars that he had given them in the places and in the manner they had told us. We told them that he was a demon and as best we could gave them to understand that if they would believe in God Our Lord and were Christians like ourselves, they would have no fear of him, nor would he dare to come and do those things to them; and that they could be certain that as long as we stayed in the land he would not dare to appear in it. They rejoiced greatly over this and lost a large part of the fear they had.

These Indians told us that they had seen the Asturian and Figueroa farther along the coast with other Indians whom we called the Fig People. All these people did not know how to measure time by the sun or the moon, nor do they have any reckoning of the month and the year; rather, they understand and recognize the difference in the seasons by when the fruits ripen, the time when the fish die,[42] and the appearance of the stars, in which they are very skilled and experienced. We were always well treated by these Indians, though we had to dig for our food and carry our loads of water and firewood. Their houses and victuals are like those of the former Indians, though they suffer much more from hunger, for they have no access to maize or acorns or nuts. We always went about naked, like them, and at night covered ourselves with deerskins. For six of the eight months we were with them we suffered greatly from hunger, for they have no fish available either. And at the end of this time the prickly pears began to ripen, and without their noticing it we went to other Indians farther on, called Maliacones; they lived a day's journey from the place the black and I reached.[43] After three days I sent him to bring Castillo and Dorantes.

And when they came we all went with the Indians who were going to eat a kind of fruit from the trees, which they live on for ten or twelve days until the prickly pears are ripe. And there they joined other Indians who are called Arbadaos; and we found these very ill and skinny and swollen-bellied, so much so that we were astonished, and the Indians with whom we had come returned by the same route. And we told them that we wished to stay with the others, which made them sad, and so we stayed in the countryside with those Indians, near their houses. And when they saw us they joined together after having talked among themselves, and each of them took each of us by the hand and led us to their houses. With these Indians we suffered more from hunger than with the others, for we ate only a couple of handfuls of that fruit in the course of a day, and it was green; it had so much juice that it burned our mouths, and since there was little water it gave the persons eating it much thirst. And such was our hunger that we bought two dogs[44] from them and in exchange gave them some nets and other things, and a hide that I used to cover myself.

I have already mentioned how we were naked everywhere in this country, and as we were not used to it, we shed our skin like snakes twice a year, and with the sun and wind developed great sores on our chests and backs, which hurt us badly because of the large loads we carried, which were very heavy and caused the cords to cut into our arms. And the land is so rugged and heavily forested that we often sought firewood in the woods, and when we had finished getting it blood would run in many places from thorns and thickets we encountered, which broke the skin wherever they touched us. Sometimes it happened that I went for wood in places where, after gathering it had cost me much blood, I could neither carry nor drag it. When I was in these difficulties, my only solace was to think

of the passion of our Redeemer Jesus Christ, and the blood he
shed for me, and to consider how much greater was the torment he suffered from the thorns than that I was then
experiencing.

I traded with these Indians by making combs for them and
also bows and arrows and nets. We made reed mats, which
are things that they have great need of, and though they know
how to make them they do not wish to work at anything,
because they are always looking for food. And when they are
occupied with this search they suffer great hunger. At other
times they made me scrape hides and soften them. And my
greatest good fortune while I was there were the days that they
gave me something to scrape, for I would scrape it very hard
and eat those scrapings, and that would suffice me for two or
three days. It also sometimes happened, both with these Indians and the ones we had left behind, that they gave us a
piece of meat, and we would eat it raw, for if we set about
roasting it the first Indian who came along would take it away
from us and eat it; and we thought that we had better not risk
it, and we ourselves were in no condition to mind whether we
ate it roasted or not and could not eat it as well as when it
was raw. This is the life that we had there, and the little food
that we earned by trading things we had made with our hands.

CHAPTER XXIII

How We Departed after
Eating the Dogs

After we ate the dogs, believing that we had some strength to continue on our way and commending ourselves to God Our Lord to guide us, we took our leave of those Indians and they pointed the way to others of their language who were near there. And as we went along it rained, and we traveled all that day with rain; and in addition to this we lost our way and came to a large wood, and we picked many cactus leaves and roasted them that night in an oven that we made; we roasted them so thoroughly that in the morning they were fit to eat. And after we had eaten them we commended ourselves to God and set off and found the path that we had lost. And when we came out of the woods we found other Indian houses, and when we reached the place we saw two women and children who were frightened of us; they were in the woods and fled from us and went to call the Indians who were nearby. And when they had come they peered at us from behind some trees, and we called to them and they approached with much fear, and after we had talked to them they told us that they were very hungry, and that there were many houses of theirs nearby and said that they would take us to them.

And that night we reached a place where there were fifty houses, and the people were startled when they saw us and showed great fear. And after they had become somewhat accustomed to us, they would touch us with their hands on our faces and body and then pass their own hands over their faces and bodies. And so we were there that night, and in the morning they brought us their sick, begging us to sign them with the cross, and they gave us such supplies as they had of food, which were cactus leaves and green prickly pears, roasted. And because of the good treatment they gave us, and because they gave us willingly and generously what they had and were happy to go without in order to give it to us, we stayed with them for several days. And while we were there others came from farther off. When they decided to leave, we told the first Indians that we wanted to go with them also. They were very unhappy about this and begged us very heartily not to go, and at last we said farewell to them and left them weeping for our departure, for they felt it very deeply.

CHAPTER XXIV

Of the Customs of the Indians
of That Land

All the Indians that we saw from the Isle of Ill Fortune to this land have the custom, from the day that their wives realize that they are pregnant, of not sleeping with them until the children have been raised for two years; and they suckle them until they are twelve years old, for by that time they have reached an age to seek food for themselves. We asked them why they reared children like this, and they said it was because of the great hunger in the land, that it happened very often, as we saw, that they went for two or three days without eating, and sometimes four days; and for this reason they let them suckle to keep them alive in times of hunger, and that otherwise even if some did survive, they would be very delicate and feeble. And if perchance some of the children fall ill, they let them die out there in the plains unless they are their own children, and all others are left behind if they cannot keep up; however, they will pick up a son or brother and carry him on their backs.

All these Indians customarily leave their wives when there is disagreement between them and marry again to whomever they please. This is among the young men; but those who have children stay with their wives and do not leave them. And when in some villages there are those who quarrel and have disputes among themselves, they strike and beat each other to the point of exhaustion and then draw apart. Sometimes the women separate them by coming between them, but men never do so; and no matter how angry they are they do not resort to bows and arrows in these fights. And after they have pummeled each other and had out their dispute, they take their houses and their wives and go and live in the plains, away from the others, until their anger has cooled. And when they have overcome their animosity and are no longer angry, they return to their village and from then on are friends, as though nothing had happened between them, nor does anyone have to make peace between them, for this is the way they settle their quarrels. And if those who have quarreled are not married they go to other neighboring tribes, who even if they are enemies receive them courteously and entertain them well and give them some of their own possessions; so that when their anger has passed they return to their village and come back rich.

All of them are warlike and are as skillful in protecting themselves against their enemies as if they had been reared in Italy[45] and in constant warfare. When they are in a place where their enemies might attack them, they erect their houses on the edge of the roughest wood and with the heaviest vegetation that they can find in the vicinity, and next to it they dig a ditch and sleep there. All the warriors are covered with small branches among which they make peepholes and are so covered and hidden that even if their enemies were right on top of them, they would not see them. And they make a very narrow path that goes into the center of the wood, and there they make a place for the women and children to sleep and at nightfall go back to light fires in their houses so that, if spies were about, they would believe that the houses were occupied. And before dawn they light those same fires again; and should their enemies reach the houses themselves, those who are in the ditch attack them and do great damage from their trenches without the enemy being able to see or find them. And when there are no woods where they can hide in this way and prepare their ambushes, they set up their houses on the plain at a place that seems most favorable to them and surround themselves with trenches covered with small branches and make their peepholes from which they shoot arrows at the other Indians; these preparations are made for night fighting.

During the time I was with the Aguenes Indians their enemies came unexpectedly at midnight and attacked them and killed three and wounded many more, so that they fled from their houses into the woods; and when they were sure that the others had left they returned home and picked up all the arrows that the others had shot and as stealthily as possible followed them; and that night they approached their houses without being heard, and very early in the morning they attacked them and killed five, not counting many others who were wounded, and caused them to flee and leave their houses and bows and all their possessions. And a short time later the women of the tribe called Queuenes came and settled the quarrel between them and made them friends, although sometimes women are the causes of war. All these people, when they have individual enemies, so long as they are not members of the same family, kill each other at night by lying in ambush and treat each other with the utmost cruelty.[46]

CHAPTER XXV

Of the Indians' Readiness to Use Arms

These people are the readiest to use arms of any I have seen in the world, for if they are in fear of their enemies they stay awake all night with their bows beside them and a dozen arrows; and when a man goes to sleep he tests his bow and if he does not find it properly strung he stretches it as much as is needful. They often come out of their houses crouched low to the ground so that they cannot be seen and look and spy about in every direction to see what is there; and if they notice something at one place, all of them are out in the open with their bows and arrows, and they stay in this state of readiness until daybreak, running to and fro where they think it necessary, or where they believe their enemies may be. When day comes they again loosen their bowstrings until they go hunting. The strings of their bows are made of deer sinews.

The way they have of fighting is to crouch low to the ground, and while they are exchanging arrows they are constantly yelling and leaping, always from one side to another, avoiding their enemies' arrows; so effective is this that they can receive little hurt in vital parts from crossbows and muskets. Indeed, the Indians laugh at them because these weapons are of no use against them in open places where they can move about easily; they are good for narrow places and on water. As for the rest, horses are the only thing that will subdue them, and the thing universally feared by the Indians. Whoever wishes to fight them must be constantly on his guard not to show weakness, or covetousness for anything they own. And while the warfare lasts they must be treated very harshly, for if they recognize fear or any sort of greed, they are people who know when the time for retaliation is at hand and gain courage from their enemies' fear.

When they have exchanged arrows in war and used up all their weapons, each side goes its own way and they do not follow each other, though one group may be large and the other small, and that is their custom. Often their bodies are pierced through by arrows, and they do not die of their wounds unless the entrails or heart are hit; rather, they heal very quickly. They see and hear more and have the sharpest senses, I believe, of any people in the world. They are very patient sufferers from hunger and thirst and cold, like folk who are more used and inured to it than others. I have wanted to tell this because, apart from the fact that all men wish to know the customs and actions of others, those who may at some time have to do with these people should know about their customs and stratagems, which may be of no little use in such cases.

CHAPTER XXVI

Of the Tribes and Their Languages

I also wish to tell of the tribes and languages that exist between the Isle of Ill Fortune and these last Indians.[47] On the Isle of Ill Fortune there are two languages: they call one of them the language of the Capoques, and the other, Han. On the mainland, opposite the island, there are other Indians called Chorrucos, and they take their name from the woods where they dwell. Farther on, along the seacoast, are others called Deaguanes. And opposite them others whose name is the Mendicas. Farther along the coast are the Queuenes. And opposite them, well inland, the Mareames; and along the coast are others called Guaycones. And opposite these, inland on the mainland, the Yguazes. And besides these are others called Atayos, and behind them others called Acubadaos, and there are many of these farther on in the same direction.

On the coast live others called Quitoles. And opposite these, well inland, the Avavares. Together with these are the Maliacones and other Cutalchiches, and others who are called Susolas and others Comos, and farther along the coast are the Camoles, and farther along the same coast are others whom we called the Fig People. All these folk have houses and villages and different languages. Among these Indians there is a language in which they call to other men by saying "Look here, hurry here," and to dogs they say "Ho." All through this land they stupefy themselves with a certain smoke[48] and will give all they have to obtain it. They also drink something that they brew from the leaves of a tree resembling an oak and toast in pots over a fire; and after it is toasted they fill the pot with water and keep it over the fire, and when that water has boiled twice they pour it into another vessel and cool it with half a gourd, and when it has a great deal of froth they drink it as hot as they can bear it; and from the time that they take it out of the pot until they drink it they are shouting, "Who wants to drink?" When the women hear these shouts they stop without daring to move, and though they may be heavily laden they dare not do anything else. And if perchance one of them moves, they insult her and beat her and very angrily spill the water that they have ready to drink and vomit up what they have drunk already, something which they do very easily and without effort.

They give the reason for this custom and say that if the women move from where they hear the shout when they are about to drink this water, something bad gets into their bodies from the water, and that it kills them within a short time. And during all the time that the water is cooking the pot must be covered. And if perchance it is uncovered and a woman passes by, they pour it out and drink no more of that water; it is yellow, and they drink it for three days without eating, and every day each man drinks an *arroba*[49] and a half of it. And when a woman is in her monthly condition she seeks food only for herself, for no other person will eat what she brings. During the time that I was with them I saw a devilish thing, and it was that I saw a man married to another man, and these are effeminates and impotent and go about covered like women and do the work of women and do not shoot arrows, and carry very heavy loads; and among these folk we saw many of them who were thus effeminate, as I have said, and they are heavier and taller than the other men; they can bear extremely heavy loads.[50]

CHAPTER XXVII

How We Moved and
Were Well Received

After we departed from those whom we left weeping, we went with the other Indians to their houses and were well received by those who lived in them, and they brought their children for us to touch their hands, and gave us a great quantity of mesquite flour.[51] This mesquite is a fruit that when it is on the tree is very bitter and somewhat resembles carobs, and it is eaten with earth and then is sweet and good to taste. The way they have of preparing it is as follows: they make a hole in the ground, as deep as each person desires, and after the fruit is tossed into this hole they grind it with a stick as thick as a man's leg, and a cubit and a half in length, until it is very well ground; and in addition to the earth that sticks to it in the hole they bring more earth and throw handfuls of it into the hole and grind the fruit for another while, and then they put it into a vessel rather like a reed basket and put in enough water to cover the fruit, so that there is water on top of it; and then the person who has ground it tastes it, and if he thinks that it is not sweet enough he asks for more earth and mixes it in, and does this until he finds it sweet; and then they all sit down around it and each one puts in his hand and takes as much as he can, and the seeds and rinds they turn out onto some hides.

And the man who has done the grinding takes them and puts them back into that basket and adds water as at first, and then they again press out the juice and water that come from it; and they again place the seeds and rinds on the hide and in this way make every grinding three or four times. And those who are present at this banquet, which for them is a very great thing, are left with very swollen bellies from the earth and water they have drunk. And the Indians made a great festivity of this for our benefit, and there were great dances and ceremonies among them all the time we were there. And when we were sleeping at night near the door of the house where we were, six men watched over each of us with great care, and no one dared to enter until the sun rose. At the point when we had decided to leave them, some women arrived from another tribe who lived farther on, and having learned from them where their houses were, we set off to find them, though they entreated us earnestly to stay another day, for the houses where we were going were far away and there was no path to them, and those women were tired, and if they rested for another day they would go with us and guide us; and so we took our leave of them. And after a short time the women who had come, along with other women from the same village, went after us; but as there were no paths in that land we soon became lost, walked for four leagues, and at the end of them came to a stream where we could drink, where we found the women who had followed us, and they told us how difficult it had been to overtake us.

We left there taking the women with us as guides and crossed a river during the afternoon, where the water was up to our chests; it was about as wide as the river in Seville[52] and had a very strong current. And at sunset we reached a hundred houses of Indians; and before we had arrived all the people who were in them came out to greet us, with such shouting that it was frightening to hear, and striking themselves hard on the thighs; they brought gourds with holes bored in them, with stones inside, which is their most festive object and one that they bring out only for dancing, or to cure, and no one dares touch them but themselves; and they say that those gourds have virtue and that they come from heaven, for there are none in that land, nor do they know where they are to be found, but the rivers bring them when they are in flood. The fear and confusion of these folk was such that some, trying to reach us before the others and touch us, squeezed us so much that they nearly killed us; and they carried us to their houses without letting our feet touch the ground, and there were so many carrying us, and they pressed us so tightly, that we got into the houses that they had made for us and did not allow them to make revelry with us that night in any way.

All that night the Indians spent in ceremonies and dances, and next morning they brought us all the folk of that village for us to touch and make the sign of the cross over them, as we had done with the others with whom we had stayed. And after this was done, they gave many arrows to the women of the other tribe who had come with their women. On the following day we left there, and all the people in the village went with us, and when we came to other Indians we were well received, just as with the former ones; and so they gave us of what they had and the deer they had killed that day. And among these Indians we saw a new custom, and it is that when they came to be healed, those who were with us took away their bow and arrows and shoes and beads, if they had any, and after having taken them away they brought the people before us to have us cure them; and when they were healed they went away very happy, saying that they were in perfect health. And so we departed from those Indians and went to others, by whom we were very well received; and they brought us their sick, who after we had signed them with the cross declared themselves to be in health, and if anyone was not cured he believed that we could cure him, and along with what the others whom we cured told them, they made so merry and held so many dances that they did not allow us to sleep.

CHAPTER XXVIII

Of Another New Custom

After we had left these folk we went to many other houses, and a new custom began at this time; and it was that though they received us very well, those who accompanied us began to behave so badly that they stole their property and ransacked their houses and left them with nothing; this distressed us very much, to see the ill treatment that was offered to those who received us so well. Also we feared that such behavior would be, or would cause, some change and outrage among them; but as we could do nothing about it, nor dare to punish those who did this, we had to endure it until there was more discipline among them; and also the very Indians who had lost their possessions, knowing how sad we were, consoled us by saying that no harm would come to us because of it, and that they were so glad to have seen us that they thought their possessions well lost, and that later they would be repaid by others who were very rich.

All during this part of the journey we were very much hampered by the large number of people who were following us and could not escape from them although we tried, for their eagerness to come and touch us was very great and their importunity so extreme that three hours would pass without our being able to persuade them to leave us alone. Next day they brought us all the people in the village, and the greater part of them were one-eyed from the white spot, and others were blind from the same cause, which astonished us. They are very well built and have excellent manners and are lighter in color than any others we had seen up to now. Here we began to see mountain ranges, and it seemed that they were in the direction of the Northern Sea;[53] and so, from the information that the Indians gave us concerning this, we believe that they are fifteen leagues from the sea. We left this place with these Indians, in the direction of the mountain ranges I have mentioned, and they took us to places where their kinfolk lived, for they did not want to take us to any place where they did not have kin and did not want their enemies to have the good fortune of seeing us, as they believed. And when we had arrived, those who were with us robbed the others; and as they knew the custom, as soon as we arrived they hid certain things, and after they had received us with great revelry and joy, they took out what they had hidden and came to give it to us. And these things were beads and red ocher and a few little bags of silver.[54]

According to the custom, we immediately gave it all to the Indians who had come with us, and when they had given it to us their dances and festivals began, and they sent to call for others from another village that was nearby, to have them come and see us; and during the afternoon all of them came and brought us beads and bows and other little things, which we also distributed. And next day, when we wished to leave, all the people wanted to take us to other friends of theirs who lived on a spur of the mountains, and they said that there were many houses and many people there and that they would give us many things; but because it was out of our way we refused to go to them and took the level land near the mountains, which we believed were not far from the coast. All the people there are very evil; and we thought it better to traverse the level land, for the folk who live farther inland are friendlier and treated us better, and we were certain that we would find the land more thickly populated and with better supplies of food. Finally, we did this because by crossing the land we saw many features of it, so that if God Our Lord deigned to save any one of us and bring him to Christian lands, he could give information and a report about it. And as the Indians saw that we were determined not to go in the direction they were taking us, they told us that in the direction we wished to go there were no people, nor prickly pears, nor anything at all to eat, and entreated us to stay there that day, and we did so.

Then they sent two Indians to look for people along that route that we wanted to take; and next day we left, taking many of them with us, and the women were loaded with water, and our authority over them was so great that none dared to drink without our leave. Two leagues from there we came upon the Indians who had gone to look for people, and they said that they had not found any; the Indians showed concern at this and again entreated us to go by way of the mountains. We refused to do it, and when they saw our determination they said farewell to us, though with much sorrow, and returned down the river to their homes. And we went on up the river and a short time later came upon two women carrying loads, who when they saw us stopped and put down their loads and brought us what they were carrying, which was maize flour, and told us that farther up the river we would find houses and many prickly pears and more of that flour.[55] And so we took our leave of them, because they were going toward the others whom we had just left. And we marched until sunset and reached a village of some twenty houses, where they received us weeping and with great sadness, for they knew that wherever we went they would all be plundered and robbed by those who came with us; and when they saw us alone they lost their fear and gave us prickly pears and nothing else.

We stayed there that night, and at daybreak the Indians who had left us on the previous day descended upon their houses. And since they caught them unawares, and confident, they stole everything they owned, not giving them a chance to hide anything; they bewailed this very much, and the thieves, to console them, told them that we were children of the sun and had power to heal the sick and to kill them, and other lies even greater than these. Since these Indians know how to tell even greater lies when they believe it is to their advantage, they told them to treat us with the greatest caution and to take care not to make us angry, and to give us everything they owned and to try to take us to places where there were many people, and that wherever we came they must rob and plunder everything that the others had, for that was the custom.

CHAPTER XXIX

How Some Indians Robbed the Others

After having informed and carefully pointed out to them what they had to do, the Indians returned and left us with these new ones; conscious of what the others had told them, they began to treat us with the same dread and reverence as the others; and we traveled with them for three days, and they brought us to a place where there were many people. And before we arrived, they sent word to tell what we were like, told the same things of us that the other Indians had taught them, and added a great deal more, for all these tribes of Indians love fantasy and are great liars, especially when they see some advantage in it. And when we came near their houses all the people came out to greet us with great joy and revelry, and among other things two of their medicine men gave us two gourds, and after that we began to take gourds with us and added to our authority with this ceremony, which is very important to them.

The Indians who had come with us ransacked their houses; but as there were many houses and few of these Indians, they could not carry everything they had taken and left half of it to go to waste. From here we continued, skirting the slope of the mountains, inland for more than fifty leagues, and at the end of them we found forty houses; and among the other things that they gave us, Andrés Dorantes had a big heavy copper bell with a face engraved on it, and they showed us that they had much copper and said that they had acquired it from other Indians who were their neighbors. And when we asked where they had acquired such a thing, they said that it had been brought from the north and that there was much of it there, and it was greatly esteemed; and we concluded that in the places where it came from there were foundries, and that they cast metal in molds. And so we left there on the following day and crossed a mountain ridge seven leagues wide, where the stones were iron slag, and at nightfall we reached many houses located on the banks of a very beautiful river. And their owners came halfway to greet us, carrying their children, and they gave us many little bags of mica and powdered antimony,[56] which they use to paint their faces; and they gave us many beads and hides from that cattle of theirs and loaded all those who were with us with everything they owned.

They ate prickly pears and nuts from pine trees; in that land there are small pine trees and their cones are the size of small eggs; but the pine nuts are better than those of Castile, for these have very thin shells, and when they are still green they grind them and make balls of them and eat them in that way; and if they are dry they grind them, together with the shells, and eat them in the form of powder. And the Indians of that part of the land who received us, after they had touched us ran back to their houses and then returned to us, and never ceased running and returning. In this way they gave us many things for our travels. It was here that they brought me a man and told me that a long time ago he had been wounded by an arrow in his right shoulder, and he had the point of the arrow over his heart; he said that it gave him great pain, and that he was always ill because of it. I touched him and could feel the point of the arrow and saw that it had pierced the gristly parts of the chest; and with a knife that I had I opened his chest as far as that place and saw that the arrow point was wedged in crosswise and extremely hard to remove; I cut again and put the knife-point into the wound and at last removed it with great difficulty.

It was very long and was made of deer bone; using my medicinal skills, I took two stitches, and after I had made them he bled very freely, and I stanched the blood with scrapings from a hide, and when I had removed the arrow point they asked me for it and I gave it to them; and the whole village came to see it, and they sent it farther inland so that the Indians who lived there could see it; and because of this they held

FIGURE 9.   Cabeza de Vaca and his companions remove an arrowhead from an Indian. Oil painting by Ettore De Grazia. (Courtesy of the De Grazia Art and Cultural Foundation)

many dances and revels such as they are wont to do. And next day I cut the two stitches for the Indian, and he was cured and there was no sign of the wound that I had made, except for something like the line on the palm of a hand; and he said that he felt no pain or any kind of discomfort. And this cure gave us fame among them everywhere in the land equal to all that those Indians could do and esteem and value. We showed them the bell we were carrying, and they told us that in the place from which it had come many sheets of that metal were buried, and that it was a thing that they held in much esteem, and that houses there were permanent; and we believe that this must be the Southern Sea,[57] for we always heard that that sea is richer than the one in the north. We left these Indians and traveled through so many kinds of folk, and with such different languages, that memory does not serve to allow one to tell of them. And some always robbed the others, and the losers as well as the winners were very happy.

We had so many people with us that there was no way we could maintain them. In those valleys that we traveled through, each of them carried a club three handbreadths long, and they all went single file, and when a hare started up (for there were many of them there) they would immediately surround it, and so many clubs fell upon it that it was wonderful to see; and in this way they passed it from one to another, which in my opinion was the finest kind of hunt imaginable, for often the hares would come right into their hands, and when we stopped at night the hares that the people had given us were so numerous that each of us had eight or ten loads of them. And the Indians who used bows did not appear before us; rather, they drew apart into the mountains to hunt deer, and when they came at night they brought five or six deer for each of us and birds and quail and other game; in short, everything that those people found and killed they placed before us, not daring to take any of it, even if they were dying of hunger, without our first making the sign of the cross over it, for that had been their custom ever since they traveled with us; and the women would bring many mats of the sort they use to make their houses, to make for each of us his own separate house with all his own people around him; and when this was done we would give orders to roast those deer and hares and everything that they had caught, and this also was done very quickly in ovens that they made for the purpose; and we would take a little of everything and give the rest to the chief of the people who had come with us, telling him to distribute it among them all.

Each one, with the part of the food assigned to him, would come to us to have us blow on it and make the sign of the cross over it, for otherwise they would not dare to eat it; and often we had three or four thousand people with us, and it was a very great effort for us to have to blow and sign with the cross the portion that each one was to eat and drink; and for many other things that they wanted to do they came and asked our permission, from which it can be seen that we received a great deal of bother. The women brought us prickly pears and spiders and worms and whatever there was, for were they to die of hunger, they would eat nothing except what we gave them. And as we traveled with them we crossed a large river that came from the north, and when we had crossed some plains thirty leagues broad we found many folk who had come from far away to greet us, and they came out to the path where we were going to pass and received us in the same manner as the others before them.

CHAPTER XXX

How the Custom of
Receiving Us Changed

After this there was a different way of receiving us, so far as plunder was concerned, for those who went out of their way to bring us something did not rob those who came with us; but after we had entered their houses they themselves would offer us everything they possessed, and the houses too; we would give them to the chiefs so that they could divide them, and those who had been dispossessed always followed us, and hence more and more people followed in order to recover their losses; and they were told to be very careful and not to hide anything that they owned, for it was impossible to do this without our knowledge, and then we would cause them all to die, for the sun told us to do it. So great were the fears with which they were imbued, that during the first days that they were with us they were always trembling, without daring to speak or raise their eyes to heaven. These Indians guided us for more than fifty leagues of empty country among very rugged mountains, and because they were so dry there was no game in them, and hence we endured great hunger and at last came to a very large river in which the water reached our chests; and from that point onward many of the people whom we brought with us began to fall ill, owing to the great hunger and difficulty with which they had crossed those mountains, which were extremely steep and rugged.

These same Indians led us to some plains at the end of the mountains, where people came from very far away to greet us and receive us as the previous Indians had done, and gave so many provisions to those who came with us that they had to leave half of them behind because they could not carry everything; and we told the Indians who had given the provisions that they must take them back and carry them away, so that they would not be left there wasted. And they said that by no means would they do it, for it was not their custom, after a thing was received, to take it back again; and so, giving it no importance, they left everything there to be wasted. To these Indians we said that we wished to go to the setting sun. And they replied that the people there were very far away. And we told them to send news to them that we were going there, and they refused to do this as courteously as they could, for those people were their enemies and they did not want us to go to them; but they dared not disobey us.

And so they sent two women, one from their tribe and another whom they were holding captive, and they sent these because women can parley even in times of war. And we followed them and stopped in a place where it had been arranged that we wait for them; but they delayed for five days, and the Indians said that they must not have found any people. We told them to take us toward the north: they replied in the same way, saying that there were no people there, only very far away, and that there was nothing to eat, nor could water be found. And we disagreed with all this and said that we wished to go there, and they continued to decline as politely as they could, and so we became angry, and one night I went out to sleep in the countryside, away from them; but then they went to where I was and stayed awake all night, terribly afraid and talking to me and telling me how frightened they were and begging us not to be angry any more, and that though they knew they would die on the way, they would take us where we wished to go. And as we still pretended to be angry to keep their fear from diminishing, a strange thing happened, and it was that on this same day many of them fell ill, and eight men died the next day. All over the land, in the places where this became known, they were so afraid of us that it seemed that the very sight of us made them almost die of fear.

They implored us not to be angry, nor to wish for any more of them to die; and they were altogether convinced that we killed them simply by wishing to. And the truth is that we felt such sorrow about this that it could not have been greater, for in addition to seeing those that were dying we feared that all of them would die, or that out of fear they would leave us all alone and that all the other folk farther on would do the same when they realized what had happened to these Indians. We beseeched God Our Lord to help us, and so all those who had fallen ill began to get well. And we saw something greatly to be wondered at, that the parents and brothers and sisters and mothers of those who died were exceedingly sorrowful to see them in that state of illness, and yet after they died they showed no emotion, nor did we see them weep nor speak together nor give any other sign of grief, nor did they dare to approach their kinfolk until we ordered them to take them away and bury them. And for more than fifteen days that we were with these people, we never saw any one of them speak with another, nor did we see them laugh nor allow any child to cry; rather, when one little girl cried they took her far away from there and, with some sharp mouse teeth, slashed her from the shoulders almost all the way down her legs.

And I, witnessing this act of cruelty and being angry about it, asked them why they did it, and they replied that it was to punish her for having cried in my presence. All these fears that they had they transmitted to all the others who were coming to see us for the first time, so that they would give us everything they had; for they knew that we would not accept anything and that we would necessarily give it all to them. These were the most obedient folk that we found in this land, and the healthiest, and they are commonly very handsome. When the sufferers had recovered and we had been there for three days, the women we had sent arrived saying that they had found very few people and that all of them had gone to hunt cattle, for it was the season for them. And we ordered those who had been ill to stay behind, and those who were well to go with us, and that after two days' travel those same two women would go with two of us to get the people and bring them to meet us on the road; this decided, all of the strongest left with us next morning and we stopped after three days, and on the following day Alonso del Castillo left with

Estebanico the black, taking the two women as guides, and the one that was a captive led them to a river that ran between mountains, where there was a village in which her father lived; and these were the first houses we saw that really looked like houses.

Castillo and Estebanico arrived there, and after having talked with the Indians, three days later Castillo came to the place where he had left us and brought five or six of those Indians, and he told how he had found real and permanent houses, and that those people ate beans and squash, and that he had seen maize.[58] This was the thing in the world that made us happiest, and we gave infinite thanks to Our Lord for it. And he said that the black would come with all the people of those houses, to wait for us on the road near there. And so we left, and after we had traveled a league and a half we came upon the black and the people who were coming to receive us, and they gave us beans and many squashes to eat and to carry water in, and cattle hides and other things. And as these people and the ones who had come with us were enemies and did not understand each others' speech, we took leave of the first group, returning to them what they had given us, and went with the new Indians; and six leagues from there, when night was falling, we reached their houses, where they made much revelry with us. We stayed there a day, and next day we left and took them with us to other permanent houses where the people ate as they did.

And from here onward there was another new custom, which was that those who learned of our coming did not come out to the roads to receive us, as the others had; rather, we found them in their houses and they had made other houses for us; and all were seated with faces turned toward the wall and heads lowered and hair covering their eyes, and with all their possessions placed in the center of the house. And from here on they began to give us many hides, and there was nothing they possessed that they did not give us. These people have the best bodies of those we saw, and the most cleverness and skill, and they were the ones who best understood and answered us when we asked questions of them, and we called

them the Cattle People because it is near there that most of
the cattle perish, and for fifty leagues along that river the Indians kill many of them. These people go about entirely naked,
like the first ones that we found. The women cover themselves
with deerskins, as a few men do, especially men who are old
and of no use in war.

It is a heavily populated land. We asked why they did not
sow maize; they replied that they were not doing so in order
not to lose the crop, for during two consecutive years the rains
had failed and the weather had been so dry that all had lost
their whole crop of maize, and they did not dare sow it again
until first there had been copious rain. And they begged us to
tell the heavens to rain, to implore them to do so, and we
promised them that we would do this. We also asked them
from where they had brought that maize, and they said from
the direction the sun set, and in that land there was maize
everywhere; but the maize closest to us was in that direction.
We asked them which was the best way to go and to describe
the road to us, for they did not wish to go there. They told us
that the way led up that river toward the north, and that for
seventeen days' journey we would find nothing to eat except
a fruit that they call *chacán* and grind between stones, and
even after this treatment it is inedible, for it is so bitter and
dry; and indeed such was the truth, for they showed it to us
there and we could not eat it. And they also told us that as
we traveled up the river we would always be among folk who
were their enemies and spoke their same language, and who
could not give us anything to eat but would receive us very
willingly and give us many cotton blankets and hides and other
things they owned; but that they still believed we ought not
to take that road under any circumstances.

Doubtful of what we should do, and which road we should
take to fit our plans best and be of most use to us, we stayed
with them for two days. They gave us beans and squash to
eat; their way of cooking them is so novel that I wish to record
it here, so that it can be seen and recognized how diverse and
strange are the devices and tactics of human beings. They are
too primitive to have cooking pots, and to cook what they wish

to eat they fill a large gourd half-full of water and put many stones into the fire, of the kind that heat most readily and accept the flame, and when they see that the stones are burning hot they take them with wooden tongs and throw them into that water in the gourd, until they make it boil with the heat that the stones contribute, and when they see that the water is boiling they throw into it whatever they need to cook; and in all this time they simply take out some stones and put in others that are burning hot, so that the water boils and cooks whatever they want, and this is the way they cook.

CHAPTER XXXI

How We Followed the Maize Road

After we had been there for two days we determined to go
and look for maize and did not want to follow the path of the
cattle because it was toward the north, and this was very much
out of our way, for we were always sure that by going toward
the setting sun we would find what we desired: and so we
continued on our way and crossed the whole country until we
came to the Southern Sea, and the fear that the Indians tried
to instill in us of the great hunger we would have to endure
(as indeed we did endure) was not sufficient to deter us for all
of the seventeen days of the journey they had told us of. During
all those days, as we traveled up the river, they gave us many
cattle hides, and we did not eat that fruit of theirs, but each
day our rations were a handful of deer fat that we tried always
to keep on hand for these emergencies. And so we passed all
the seventeen days and at the end of them we crossed the river
and traveled for another seventeen, in the direction of the
sunset, through plains and between the very high mountains
that are there; we found some people there who eat nothing
but powdered straw for the third part of the year, and because
when we passed through it was that time of year, we also had
to eat it until those days of journeying ended, when we found
permanent houses where much maize was stored, and they
gave us a great quantity of it and its flour, and squash and
beans and cotton blankets, and we loaded everything onto
those people who had brought us there, who with all these
supplies returned the happiest folk in the world.

We gave many thanks to God Our Lord for bringing us there,
where we found so much food. Among these houses were some
made of earth, and all the others are made of reed mats; and
from there we went on for a hundred leagues and always found

permanent houses and good supplies of maize and beans. And they gave us many deer and many cotton blankets, better than those of New Spain. They also gave us many beads and some corals that are found in the Southern Sea and many very fine turquoises that they have, which come from the north; and in a word, the people here gave us everything they had, and they gave me five emeralds[59] made into arrow points, and with these arrows they perform their rites and dances. And, as it seemed to me that they were very good, I asked them where they had procured them, and they said that they were brought from some very high mountains that are toward the north, and that they bought them in exchange for plumes and parrot feathers; and they said that there were towns there with many people and very large houses.

Among these Indians we saw women more modestly arrayed than in any other part of the Indies that we had seen. They wear cotton shifts that reach to their knees, and over them a tunic with half sleeves, and skirts of dressed deerskin that touch the ground, and they soap these with a kind of root that makes them very clean, and so they are very well kept; they are open in front and tied with thongs; they wear shoes. All these people came to us to be touched and signed with the cross and were so insistent in this that we found it very hard to bear, for all of them, sick and well, wanted us to make the sign of the cross over them. It often happened that some of the women who were traveling with us gave birth, and then they would bring us the baby as soon as it was born to have us touch it and sign it with the cross. They always went along with us until they had turned us over to others, and among all these folk there was a firm conviction that we had come from heaven. While we were with these people we would march all day until night without eating and ate so little that they were astonished. They never observed fatigue in us, and truly, we were so inured to hardship that we did not feel it either.

We behaved to them with great authority and gravity and, to preserve this impression, spoke little. The black talked with them constantly, found out about the ways we wanted to go and what towns there were and the things we wished to know. We passed through a great number and diversity of languages; in all of them God our Lord favored us, for they always understood us and we them. And so we would ask and they would reply by signs as if they understood our language and we theirs, for even though we knew six languages we could not make use of them everywhere, for we found more than a thousand differences. In all these lands the Indians who were at war with others quickly became friends so that they could come and greet us and bring us everything they had, and thus we left the whole land at peace. And we told them by signs, so that they would understand, that there was a man in heaven whom we called God, who had created heaven and earth, and that we adored him and had him as our lord, and that we did what he commanded us to do, and that from his hand came all good things; and that if they would do this they would be much the better for it. And we found in them such a disposition to believe, that if there had been a language in which we could have understood each other perfectly we would have left them all Christians. We gave them to understand this as best we could, and from then on when the sun rose, with a great cry they would hold up their joined hands to heaven and then would pass them all over their bodies and would do the same when the sun set. They are a well disposed and intelligent folk, apt to follow any doctrine were it well prepared.

CHAPTER XXXII

How They Gave Us Hearts of Deer

In the village[60] where they gave us the emeralds, they gave Dorantes more than six hundred hearts of deer, opened, of which they always have a great abundance for their food; and so we called it the Village of the Hearts, and it is the gateway to many provinces that are on the Southern Sea; and if those who go to look for the sea do not pass through here they will be lost, for there is no maize on the coast and they eat powdered herbs and straw, and fish that they take in the sea with rafts, for they are too primitive to have canoes. The women cover their private parts with grass and straw. They are a very timid and dejected people. We believe that near the coast, along the route of those villages that we found, are more than a thousand leagues of populated country and good supplies of food, for the people sow beans and maize three times a year. There are three kinds of deer, and those of one kind are as large as yearling bulls in Castile; there are permanent houses that they call *bohíos*,[61] and they have a poison that comes from some trees of the size of apple trees, and they have only to pick the fruit and smear it on the arrow; and if it has no fruit they break off a branch and do the same with the milky sap these trees contain.

There are many of these trees, which are so poisonous that if the people bruise its leaves and wash them in some nearby water, all the deer and other animals that drink of it will soon burst. We stayed in this village three days, and a day's journey from there was another village in which we were caught in such a rainstorm that, because a river rose very high, we could not cross and stayed for fifteen days. During this time Castillo saw a buckle from a sword belt hanging around the neck of an Indian, with a horseshoe nail sewed to it; he took it from him and we asked him what that was, and the Indians told us that it had come from heaven. We asked further, who had brought it from there? and they replied that those who brought it were some men who wore beards like us, and who had come from heaven and reached that river, and that they had horses and lances and swords, and that they had wounded two of their people with lances. And feigning as much indifference as possible, we asked them, what had become of those men? and they answered that they had gone to the sea and thrust their lances under water, and that they had also gone under the water, and that later the Indians saw them floating on the water in the direction of the setting sun.

We offered many thanks to God Our Lord for what we had heard, for we had despaired of hearing news of Christians, and on the other hand we were very doubtful and sad, believing that those people were merely men who had come by sea to explore; but at last, as we had such undeniable news of them, we proceeded with more haste and always found more news of Christians. And we told the Indians that we were seeking them to tell them not to kill Indians, nor to make slaves of them, nor to take them from their lands, nor to do them any other harm at all, and they rejoiced very much to hear this. We traveled over much territory and found all of it uninhabited because those who dwelt in it were fleeing to the mountains, not daring to have houses or cultivate the land for fear of the Christians. It made us extremely sad to see how fertile the land was, and very beautiful, and very full of springs and rivers, and to see every place deserted and burned, and the people so thin and ill, all of them fled and hidden. And as they did not sow, they were so hungry that they lived off the bark and roots of trees. We suffered in some degree from this hunger, for they could hardly supply us when they were so unhappy that it seemed they wished to die.

They brought us blankets that they had hidden for fear of the Christians and gave them to us, and even told us how on many occasions the Christians had entered the land and destroyed and burned the villages and carried off half the men and all the women and children, and that those who had man-

aged to escape from their hands were wandering and in flight.
We saw that they were so frightened, not daring to stay in any
place, and that they neither wanted nor were able to sow crops
or cultivate the land but rather were determined to let themselves die, and they thought this was better than waiting to
be treated with such cruelty as they had endured until now;
and they showed great pleasure in us, though we feared that
once we reached the Indians who had a frontier with the Christians, and were making war on them, these others would treat
us ill and make us pay for what the Christians had done to
them. But as God Our Lord was pleased to bring us to them,
they began to dread and revere us as the others had done, and
even a little more, which surprised us no little; which clearly
shows that all these people, if they are to be brought to be
Christians and into obedience of Your Imperial Majesty, must
be led by good treatment, and that this is a very sure way, and
no other will suffice.

These Indians brought us to a village[62] that is on the cusp
of a mountain, and very difficult to reach; and there we found
many people together, gathered for fear of the Christians. They
received us very well and offered us everything they had and
gave us more than two thousand loads of maize, which we in
turn gave to those poverty-stricken and hungry folk who had
brought us there. And next day we sent forth four messengers
throughout the land, as we were accustomed to do, to call and
convoke as many people as they could to a village three days'
journey from there. And when we had done this, next day we
set off with all the people who were there and always found
traces and signs where Christians had slept, and at midday we
encountered our messengers, who told us that they had found
no one, for all the people were hidden in the woods, fleeing
so that the Christians would not kill or make slaves of them,
and that on the previous night they had seen the Christians
as they spied on them from behind some trees, watching what
they were doing, and that they had seen how they were leading
many Indians in chains. On hearing this the Indians who had
come with us were greatly alarmed, and some of them returned
to warn the land that Christians were coming; many more

would have done this had we not told them not to do it and not to be afraid, and with this news they felt reassured and rejoiced greatly. At that time Indians from a hundred leagues away were with us, and we could not persuade them to return to their homes; to reassure them we slept there that night, and next day we traveled on and slept on the way. And on the following day those whom we had sent as messengers guided us to where they had seen the Christians, and at the hour of vespers we saw clearly that they had spoken the truth and realized that they were mounted men, for we saw the stakes to which the horses had been tied. From this place where we learned of Christians, which is called the river of Petatlán, to the river that Diego de Guzmán reached,[63] it may be some eighty leagues. And from there to the village where we had the flood, twelve leagues. And from there to the Southern Sea, some twelve leagues. All through this land, where there are mountains, we saw abundant signs of gold and antimony, iron, copper, and other metals. The place where the permanent houses are is very warm, so much so that the weather is hot in January. From there to the southern part of the land, which is uninhabited as far as the Northern Sea, it is very wretched and poor, where we suffered great and incredible hunger, and those who live and wander through that land are terribly cruel folk and very evil in intention and customs. The Indians who live in the permanent houses, and those behind them, have no regard for gold and silver, nor do they believe that any use can be made of them.

CHAPTER XXXIII

How We Saw Traces of Christians

After we had seen undeniable traces of Christians and realized that we were so close to them, we offered many thanks to God Our Lord for being pleased to rescue us from so sad and miserable a captivity; and the pleasure that we felt can be imagined by anyone who thinks about the length of time we had been in that land and the perils and hardships we had endured. That night I appealed to one of my companions to go after the Christians, who were moving toward the region where we had left the land at peace, and it was three days' journey. He as well as the others took this ill, excusing themselves on the grounds of exhaustion and toil; and although any one of them could have done it better than I, for they were stronger and younger, when I saw their unwillingness I took the black and eleven Indians with me next morning and, judging from the traces that I found by following the Christians, I passed through three places where they had spent the night; and that day I walked ten leagues.

And next morning I overtook four mounted Christians,[64] who were thunderstruck to see me so strangely dressed and in the company of Indians. They went on staring at me for a long space of time, so astonished that they could neither speak to me nor manage to ask me anything. I told them to take me to their captain; and so we went to a place half a league away where Diego de Alcaraz, their captain, was; and after speaking to me he told me that he was completely lost there, because for many days he had not been able to capture any Indians, and that he did not know where to go, for his people had begun to feel need and hunger. I told him how Dorantes and Castillo had stayed behind, that they were ten leagues away with many folk who had brought us there. And then he sent three horsemen and fifty of the Indians whom they had brought with them, and the black returned with them to guide them, and I stayed there and asked them to give me a certified statement of the year and month and day that I had arrived there, and the way in which I had come, and they did so. There are thirty leagues from this river to the town of the Christians, which is called San Miguel[65] and is under the authority of the province named New Galicia.

CHAPTER XXXIV

How I Sent for the Christians

After five days Andrés Dorantes and Alonso del Castillo arrived with the men who had gone after them, and they brought with them more than six hundred persons belonging to that tribe whom the Christians had forced to go into the thickets and hide in the land; and the Indians who had come thus far with us had persuaded them to come out of the forests and had turned them over to the Christians, and had dismissed all the other folk whom they had brought there. And when they reached the place where I was, Alcaraz begged me to send for and call upon the people of the towns near the river, who were hiding in the forests of the land, and command them to bring us food, though this request was unnecessary because they were always careful to bring us everything they could. And so we sent our messengers to call them, and six hundred persons came and brought us all the maize they could lay their hands on; they brought it in pots sealed with clay, in which they had buried and concealed it, and they brought us everything else they owned; but we refused to take any of it except the food and gave all the rest to the Christians to divide among themselves.

And after this we had many and great altercations with the Christians, because they wanted to make slaves of the Indians we had brought; we were so angry that when we departed we left behind many Turkish-style bows that we had brought and many pouches and arrows, among them the five that had emeralds, for we forgot them and thus lost them. We gave the Christians many hides from the Indian cows and other things that we had brought; we had great trouble persuading the Indians to return home and to feel safe there and to plant their maize. They wanted nothing but to go with us until they had

FIGURE 10.   Cabeza de Vaca in New Spain, followed by Indians. Oil painting by Ettore De Grazia. (Courtesy of the De Grazia Art and Cultural Foundation)

left us with other Indians, as their custom was, for if they returned without doing this they were afraid that they would die, and because they were with us they feared neither the Christians nor their lances. The Christians were angry at this, and had their interpreter tell them that we were men of their race and that we had been lost for a long time, that we were unlucky and cowardly people, and that they were the masters of that land, whom the Indians must obey and serve. But the Indians paid little or no heed to what they were told; rather, they talked with one another saying that the Christians were lying, for we came from where the sun rises and they from where it sets; and that we cured the sick and they killed the healthy; and that we had come naked and barefoot and they well dressed and on horses and with lances; and that we did not covet anything, rather we returned everything that they gave us and were left with nothing, and the only aim of the others was to steal everything they found, and they never gave anything to anyone; and so they told all our deeds and praised them, in contrast to the others.

And this same reply they gave to the Christians' interpreter and also to the other Indians by means of a language that was common to them, which we did not understand; those who use it are properly called *Primahaitu*,[66] which is as if we were to say Basques; and we found this language used over more than four hundred leagues that we traveled, with no other in all those lands. Finally, we never could make the Indians believe that we were like the other Christians, and with much toil and importunity we made them return to their homes and commanded them to feel safe and secure and establish their villages, and to plant and cultivate the land, which was overgrown with thickets because it had been uninhabited; it is undoubtedly the best land in these Indies and the most fertile and abounding in supplies of food, and they sow three times a year. They have many fruits and very beautiful rivers and many other very good sources of water. There are abundant indications and signs of gold and silver mines; the people there are very well disposed; they serve Christians (those who are their friends) very willingly.

They are very friendly, much more than the people of Mexico, and finally the land itself has every essential to be very good. Once we had dismissed the Indians, they told us that they would do as we commanded and would settle their villages if the Christians would leave them alone; and I say, and hold it to be very certain, that if they do not do so it will be the Christians' fault. After we had sent off the Indians in peace, thanking them for the hardships they had endured with us, the Christians delivered us under guard to a certain Zebreros, a justice of the peace, and two other officials who were with him. These led us through forests and empty lands in order to keep us from conversing with Indians and from either seeing or hearing what they in fact had done. From this fact appears how often men's thoughts are frustrated, for we wanted only to seek freedom for the Indians, and when we thought we had done so the exact opposite occurred, for the Spaniards had agreed to fall upon those whom we had sent away reassured and in peace. And as they thought, so they acted; they led us through those forests for two days, without water, lost and unable to find a road, and all of us thought we would perish of thirst, and seven men died of it; and many friendly Indians whom the Christians had brought with them could not reach the place where we found water that night until the next day at noon. And we marched twenty-five leagues with them, more or less, and at the end of them reached a town of friendly Indians, and the justice who had brought us left us there and went on another three leagues to a town called Culiacán, where Melchor Díaz resided, who was the mayor as well as captain of that province.[67]

CHAPTER XXXV

How the Mayor Received Us Well
on the Night We Arrived

As the mayor had been advised of our departure and arrival, he set off that night and came to the place where we were and wept freely with us, praising God Our Lord because He had used so much mercy toward us; the mayor spoke to us and treated us very well, and on behalf of the governor, Nuño de Guzmán, and himself offered us everything he possessed and could do, and showed much indignation at the poor reception and treatment that we had encountered from Alcaraz and the others; and we were convinced that if he had been there he would have prevented what was done to us and to the Indians. And after that night was over, next day we set forth, and the mayor entreated us earnestly to stay there and said that we would be doing very great service to God and to Your Majesty, because the land was bare of inhabitants and without cultivation and very much destroyed, and the Indians had hidden and fled into the forests and did not wish to come and settle in their villages; and he said that we should have them sent for and command them, on behalf of God and Your Majesty, to come and settle on the plains and cultivate the land. This idea seemed to us to be very difficult to put into operation, for we had not brought any of our Indians or any of those who customarily accompanied us and instructed us in these matters.

At last we decided to entrust this suggestion to two Indians of those who had been brought as captives, who were of the same tribe as those of the land; these two had been with the Christians when we first reached them and had seen the people who came with us and knew how great was the authority and control over them that we had brought and exercised in all that land, and the wonders that we had done and the sick folk we had cured, and many other things. And with these Indians we sent others from the village, to go together and call the Indians who were up in the mountains, and those of the river of Petatlán where we had found the Christians, and to tell them to come to us because we wished to speak with them. And so that they would feel safe and the others would come, we gave them a gourd of the kind that we carried in our hands (which was our chief insignia and a proof of high estate); and they went with this and wandered about for seven days, and at the end of that time they returned and brought with them three chiefs of the folk who were hiding in the mountains and brought fifteen men with them and brought us beads and turquoises and feathers. And the messengers told us that they had not found the natives of the river where we had come forth, for the Christians had caused them to flee into the forests again.

And Melchor Díaz told the interpreter to speak to the Indians as from us and tell them that we came on behalf of God who is in heaven, and that we had wandered through the world for many years telling all the people we had found to believe in God and serve Him, for He was lord of everything that is in the world. And that He gave rewards and compensated those who were good and meted out eternal punishment by fire to evil men, and that when the good died He took them to heaven, where no one ever died or was hungry or cold or thirsty, or in any other need at all, but instead in the greatest glory imaginable. And those who did not wish to believe or obey His commandments, He cast underground in the company of demons and in great fire, which was never-ending but would torment them forever, and that in addition to this, if they wished to be Christians and serve God in the way we commanded, that the Christians would consider them as brothers and would treat them very well, and that we would give orders that the Christians should do no harm to them or take them away from their lands but rather be great friends of theirs; but if they did not wish to do this the Christians would treat them very badly and would carry them off to other lands as slaves.

To this they replied to the interpreter that they would be very good Christians and serve God. And when they were asked whom they adored and sacrificed to, and to whom they prayed for water for their maize fields and their own health, they answered, to a man in heaven. We asked them what his name was and they said it was Aguar, and they believed that he had created the whole world and everything in it. We again asked them how they knew this. And they responded that their fathers and grandfathers had told them so, that they had known about this for a long time, and that he sent water and all good things. We told them that we called the being they were speaking of God, and that they must call Him so and serve and adore Him as we commanded, and they would be much better off for it. They replied that they understood all of it very well, and that they would do so. And we commanded them to descend from the mountains and come safely and in peace, and to settle the land and build their houses, and that among these houses they must make one for God, and place a cross at the entrance like the one we had there; and that when Christians came there, they must go out to meet them with crosses in their hands, without bows and without weapons, and must take them to their houses and feed them with whatever they had to eat, and in this way the Christians would do them no harm but rather be their friends. And they said that they would do as we commanded. And the captain gave them blankets and treated them very well, and so they returned taking with them the two Indians who had been captives and had gone as messengers. This happened in the presence of the scribe they had there, and many witnesses.

CHAPTER XXXVI

How We Caused Churches to Be Built in That Land

When all the Indians had departed, those of that province, who were friends of the Christians, came to see us because they had heard of us and brought us beads and feathers. And we commanded them to build churches and place crosses in them, for until then they had not done it. And we had the children of the important chiefs brought to us and had them baptized. And then the captain rendered homage to God, promising not to make or allow any raids nor to take slaves in that land and among those people whom we had reassured, and said that he would keep and enact this until His Majesty and the governor, Nuño de Guzmán, or the viceroy in his name, should establish what was most to the service of God and His Majesty. And after the children were baptized we departed for the city of San Miguel, where as soon as we arrived Indians came to tell us that many folk were coming down from the mountains and settling on the plain, and making churches and crosses and doing everything that we had commanded; and every day we had news of how this was being done and more fully accomplished.

And after we had been there for fifteen days, Alcaraz came with the Christians who had gone on that raid, and they told the captain how the Indians came down from the mountains and settled on the plain, and they found villages with many people in them that earlier had been uninhabited and deserted, and that the Indians came out to greet them with crosses in their hands and took them to their homes and gave them whatever they had, and they slept with them that night. Thunderstruck by this new situation, and the fact that the Indians told them how they were now safe, he ordered his men to do them no harm, and so they took their leave. May God Our Lord in His infinite mercy resolve that in Your Majesty's lifetime and under your power and dominion, these people may come to be truly and willingly subject to the true Lord who created and redeemed them. We are convinced that it will be so, and that Your Majesty will be the one to carry it out. It will not be so very difficult to do, for in the two thousand leagues that we traveled by land and sea, in the boats and during the other ten months when, after having ceased to be captives, we traveled continually through the land, we found no sacrifices nor idolatry. During this time we crossed from sea to sea and, by the evidence that we managed to obtain with much labor, from one coast to another, which at its widest may be as much as two hundred leagues, we succeeded in finding out that on the southern coast there are pearls and many riches, and that all the richest and best of everything in the land is near there.

We stayed in the city of San Miguel until the fifteenth day of May; and the reason why we stayed so long was that from there to the city of Compostela, where Governor Nuño de Guzmán resided, it is a hundred leagues and all is sparsely populated and enemy country, and people had to go with us; and so twenty mounted men accompanied us for forty leagues, and from there on six Christians came with us, bringing five hundred Indians who had been enslaved. And when we reached Compostela the governor received us very well and gave us clothing from his own supplies, which I could not wear for many days, nor could we sleep except on the floor; and after ten or twelve days we left for Mexico City and all along the way were well treated by the Christians, and many came out to the roads to see us and gave thanks to God for having delivered us from so many perils. We reached Mexico City on a Sunday, one day before the eve of the feast of Saint James the Apostle, where we were very well treated by the viceroy and by the Marqués del Valle[68] and received with much pleasure, and they gave us clothing and offered us everything they had, and on Saint James's Day there were a fiesta and jousting with canes and bullfights.

CHAPTER XXXVII

Of What Befell When I
Decided to Return

After we had rested in Mexico City for two months I decided to return to these realms, and when I went to take ship in the month of October a storm came up that capsized the ship, and it sank. And when I saw this I decided to let the winter pass, for in those parts it is very bad weather for sailing; and after the winter was over, at Lententide Andrés Dorantes and I left Mexico City for Veracruz to take ship and stayed there waiting for favorable weather until Palm Sunday, when we went aboard a ship and stayed on it for more than fifteen days awaiting good weather. And the ship we were in was leaking badly. I left it and went to another ship among those preparing to sail, and Dorantes stayed in the other. And on the tenth of April three ships departed from the port and sailed together for a hundred and fifty leagues; on the way two of the ships were taking in much water, and one night we lost their provisions because the pilots and mates (as later appeared) dared not go on with their ships and returned to the port from which they had sailed without our knowing it or hearing from them again; and we continued our voyage. And on the fourth day of May we reached the port of Havana, which is on the island of Cuba, where we stayed waiting for the other two ships in the belief that they were coming, until the second day of June when we left there, greatly fearing an encounter with the French, who a few days before had captured three of our ships.

And when we reached the island of Bermuda we were overtaken by a storm such as strikes everyone who passes through, as the people there say, and for a whole night gave ourselves up for lost. And it pleased God that when morning

FIGURE 11.   Havana Bay, ca. 1615. Cabeza de Vaca reached this port on 4 May 1537, on his return voyage to Spain.

came the storm abated, and we continued our voyage. Twenty-nine days after we left Havana, we had sailed for a thousand and a hundred leagues, which they say is the distance between there and the Azores. And next day, passing by the island that they call Cuervo, we sighted a French ship; at about noon it began to follow us with a caravel that it was towing, taken from the Portuguese, and it pursued us; that afternoon we sighted nine other sail, and they were so far away that we could not tell whether they were Portuguese or some of the same ships that were pursuing us. And when dusk was falling the Frenchman was a cannon-shot's length from our ship, and after dark we changed course in order to escape; but as the ship was so close to us it saw us and followed our course, and we did this three or four times and the French ship could have captured us had it wished but left the matter until the morning.

It pleased God that when dawn came we and the Frenchman were together, surrounded by the nine sail that I have said we had seen on the previous afternoon; we recognized them as belonging to the Portuguese fleet, and I gave thanks to Our Lord for having saved me from the hardships of the land and the perils of the sea. And the Frenchman, recognizing the fleet of Portugal, cut loose the caravel that it was towing, which was loaded with blacks, and which it had brought along so that we would believe they were Portuguese and wait for them. And when it was cut loose the French ship told the master and pilot of the fleet that we were French and were following the same course as they. This said, the ship put sixty men to the oars and so, both by rowing and by sail, began to move away and sailed at incredible speed. And the caravel that it had cut loose went to the galleon and told the captain that our ship and the other were French, and as our ship reached the galleon and as the whole fleet could see that we were approaching them, they were convinced that we were French and drew themselves up in battle order and started toward us. And when we came near them we saluted. Once they learned that we were friends they realized that they had been tricked, because that pirate had escaped by telling them that we were French and part of their company, and so four caravels went after him. And when the galleon came up to us, after we had saluted them, the captain, Diego de Silveira, asked us where we came from and what our cargo was. We answered that we were coming from New Spain and carried silver and gold. And he asked us how much we might be carrying. The master told him, about three hundred thousand castellanos. The captain replied in Portuguese, "By my faith, you are very rich, but you have a bad ship and worse artillery; what a rich morsel that whoreson pirate of a Frenchman has lost, by God! Now that you have escaped, follow me and do not lose me, for with God's help I will bring you into Castile."[69] And a short time later the caravels that had followed the Frenchman returned, because they thought that he was sailing at great speed, and they did not want to leave the fleet, which was escorting three ships laden with spices. And so we arrived at the island of Terceira, where we rested for fifteen days, recovering from the voyage and awaiting another ship that was coming laden from

India, part of the group of three ships that the fleet was escorting. And after the fifteen days had passed we left there
with the fleet and reached the port of Lisbon on the ninth day
of August, the Eve of Saint Lawrence, in the year one thousand
and five hundred and thirty-seven. And because it is a true
report, as I have said earlier in this account, I signed it with
my name: Cabeza de Vaca.

The account from which this book is taken was signed with
his name and his coat of arms.[70]

CHAPTER XXXVIII

What Befell the Others Who
Went to the Indies

Now that I have recounted all of the above concerning the
voyage and our entrance and departure from the land until
our return to these realms, I also wish to make mention and
report on what the ships did, and on the people who remained
in them. I have not mentioned this before because we never
heard anything about them until after our return, for we found
many people from those ships in New Spain and others here
in Castile, from whom we learned what had happened and
how everything turned out for them. After our departure the
three ships—for the other had already been lost off the rugged
coast—were in great danger, and nearly a hundred persons
stayed in them with few provisions. Among them were ten
married women, and one of them told the governor many
things that happened to him on the voyage before they occurred; and when he was preparing to explore the country she
told him not to do so, for she believed that neither he nor any
who went with him would ever leave that land, and if someone
did escape it would be because God would do mighty miracles
for him; but she believed that few would escape or none. And
then the governor answered her that he and all those who
went with him were going to fight and conquer many and very
strange peoples and lands. And that he was very certain that
many would die in the conquest, but that those who were left
would be lucky and would be very rich, because he had heard
of the riches that were in that land.

And he said more; he beseeched her to tell him about
the things she had said, past and present: who had told them
to her? She answered and said that a Moorish woman of

Hornachos[71] had told it to her in Castile, that she had reported it to us before we left Castile, and that the whole voyage had happened just as she had told us. And after the governor had left Caravallo, who was a native of the town of Huete in Cuenca, to be his lieutenant and captain of all the ships and people he was leaving behind, we separated from them, and the governor left orders that all should gather at the ships in any way they could, set sail in the direction of Pánuco, and sail constantly hugging the shore and seeking the harbor as best they could, so that when they found it they could stop there and wait for us. At the time when all of them gathered in the ships, they say that people who were there saw and heard that woman saying very clearly to the other women that, because their husbands were going to explore the interior and were placing their persons in such peril, they should by no manner of means count on them, and that they should look for the men they were going to marry, because that was what she was going to do; and so it was done, for she and the others either married or served as concubines for those who remained on the ships. And after we had left there the ships hoisted sail and continued on their way, did not find the harbor in the direction they were sailing, and so turned back.

And five leagues to the north of where we had disembarked they found the harbor, which extended seven or eight leagues into the land and was the same that we had discovered, where we had found the cases from Castile that I mentioned above, and in which were the bodies of the dead men, who were Christians. And in that harbor and along that coast the three ships, and the other that came from Havana with the brigantine, searched for us for almost a year, and as they did not find us they went to New Spain. This port that I have mentioned is the best in the world, extends seven or eight leagues into the land, and is six fathoms deep at the entrance, and nearer land five fathoms deep. The floor of the port is sandy and inside it there are no waves nor any bad storm, and as the ships that can fit inside it are very numerous, it has much fish. It is a hundred leagues from Havana, which is a town of Christians in Cuba, and is directly north of that town, and there are always gentle winds and ships can pass to and fro from one place to the other in four days, for the ships can come and go under the best of conditions.

And now that I have reported on the ships, it would be well to tell who were those men, and from what part of these realms, whom Our Lord was pleased to save from these travails. The first is Alonso del Castillo Maldonado, a native of Salamanca, son of Doctor Castillo and Doña Aldonza Maldonado. The second is Andrés Dorantes, son of Pablo Dorantes, a native of Béjar and resident of Gibraleón. The third is Alvar Núñez Cabeza de Vaca, son of Francisco de Vera and grandson of Pedro de Vera who won the Canary Islands, and his mother was named Doña Teresa Cabeza de Vaca, a native of Jerez de la Frontera. The fourth is called Estebanico; he is a black Moor, a native of Azamor.[72]

Deo gracias[73]

APPENDIX A

Note on the Text

The text offered in this edition is of considerable importance to the historiography and cultural history of America, and as such it has enjoyed for centuries a broad international circulation. Normally this *Relación*, its original title, was accompanied by its author's *Comentarios*. This was done for the first time in the 1555 edition and has become the editorial norm. On this occasion I have preferred not to combine the two texts. My reasons for doing so are many. First of all, the *Comentarios* deal with matters very different from those that appear in the *Relación*. Cabeza de Vaca's second work recounts his failed activities as governor of Paraguay, as well as the charges brought against him by the Crown when he returned to Spain as a prisoner. Moreover, because the *Comentarios* were edited by the scribe Pedro Hernández, the two texts were written in necessarily different ways. Furthermore, we do not know with any certainty to what extent Núñez participated in preparing the *Comentarios*. And when we consider the problem of its authorship, the later work necessarily appears as a second-degree version, placed in a context of quarrels and personal claims. These traits in themselves weaken the possibility of an immediate and coherent correlation between the two narratives.

In addition to the editorial hand, the narrative voice that we hear in the *Comentarios* is not clearly identifiable. In more concrete terms, the later narrative is dominated by different kinds of opinions and information. Careful inspection of the text reveals a litigious and argumentative structure fundamentally connected with the large body of documents and proofs used to refute accusations against Cabeza de Vaca as a result of his ill-starred governing activities in Río de la Plata. In more than one sense, the *Comentarios* are a carefully constructed apologia for the mission that Núñez attempted to carry out in those faraway South American regions.

The differences I have indicated do not entirely negate the links between the *Relación* and the *Comentarios;* however, these connections are more clearly apparent in the prologues than in the texts themselves. Other disparities are noticeable even without a careful comparison of the texts. We can observe, for example, that the scribe's version never achieves the stark and somewhat breathless expression so obvious in the *Naufragios*, a type of expression that even at first sight is different from the careful and correct text characteristic of the *Comentarios*. Taken as a whole, the later work completely lacks the autobiographical emotion transmitted to us by the hardships and wanderings described in the *Relación*. Indeed, it is those dimensions of the text that often plumb the depths of the human condition and make it genuinely memorable. For this reason I believe that the work deserves a presentation that emphasizes its uniqueness.

It is in the confusion of expeditions and exploratory ventures—so frequent in the sixteenth century—that Alvar Núñez Cabeza de Vaca's personality first acquires true historical importance. Núñez tells us in the opening lines of his memorable *Relación* that "On the seventeenth of June in the year fifteen hundred and twenty-seven, Governor Pánfilo de Narváez sailed from the port of Sanlúcar de Barrameda with authority and orders from Your Majesty. . . . The officers he took (for mention must be made of them) were those whose names follow: Cabeza de Vaca, as treasurer and chief officer of justice . . ." But the biographical information we so far possess about Núñez's life is not sufficient to explain convincingly how this junior officer, with a modest amount of military experience, gained access to official positions that suddenly gave him responsibilities of considerable importance. The services he had performed for the duke of Medina Sidonia do not appear to have guaranteed a promotion of this kind. Nor is there satisfactory proof that the duke took an interest in Cabeza de Vaca's aspirations. What we can logically suppose is that his rise resulted from family connections. My own researches confirm that Maestro Luis Cabeza de Vaca, count of Pernia, was one of the founding members of the Royal and Supreme Council of the Indies. In addition to his position of councillor, he had been bishop of the Canary Islands and a tutor of Charles V; in later years he would become bishop of Salamanca and Palencia. I do not think it far-fetched to suppose that family connections of this kind eased Núñez's access to posts in the Indies that, though certainly not of high administrative rank, could serve as useful stepping-stones to more important appointments. But the information we possess about Núñez's person is spotty and always subject to contradictory opinions. In his case, as in that of many of his contemporaries, we may know more about the circumstances than about the person himself.

As for Cabeza de Vaca, almost the only documents that cast incontrovertible light on his personality are the *Relación* and *Comentarios*, together with the evidence that was assembled to defend his person before the Council of the Indies.[1] Thanks to the conscientious investigations of Hipólito Sancho de Sopranis in Andalusian archives, we know today with some certainty that Alvar Núñez was born around 1492 in Jerez de la Frontera, in Andalusia, and not in Seville as has so often been stated.[2] We also know that he must have spent his childhood and adolescence in Jerez. De Sopranis's data do not exclude the possibility that he may have lived in Seville after his infancy. But there is no doubt today that almost all his relatives were from Jerez and its environs; he refers to them proudly at the end of his *Relación*. There, referring to himself, he says, "The third is Alvar Núñez Cabeza de Vaca, son of Francisco de Vera and grandson of Pedro de Vera who won the Canary Islands, and his mother was named Doña Teresa Cabeza de Vaca, a native of Jerez de la Frontera."

According to the documentary evidence unearthed by de Sopranis, Núñez and his siblings were orphaned at an early age and were placed in the care of their paternal aunt and uncle, Pedro de Vera and Beatriz Figueroa. It is often repeated that the surname of Cabeza de Vaca was conferred by Sancho of Navarre on the shepherd Martín Alhaja—the supposed ancestor of Núñez's mother—because he had marked with a cow's head a path used by the Christians to attack the Moors during the battle of Las Navas de Tolosa on 2 July 1212. No known documentary sources confirm this account. However, the American diplomat Thomas Buckingham Smith—the first translator of Cabeza de Vaca's *Relación* into English in 1851—refers to a partial *Cronología de la noble y antigua familia de Cabeza de Vaca* (1642). It was apparently a document of very debatable value. Not a few writers have attempted to describe Núñez's childhood and adolescence as a period of privations and despair. But according to estate inventories, deeds, and powers of attorney attested to by official scribes, Núñez's childhood must have been quite comfortable, for his family enjoyed a fairly secure financial position that allowed them to hold property both in Andalusia and the Canaries. We may also fairly suppose, given his family's relative prosperity, that he must have had the best education that Jerez could offer. In any case, if some of the historical data concerning Cabeza de Vaca lend themselves to several interpretations, it is because a number of persons named Alvar Núñez are registered in documents of the period.[3] There are sufficient documentary proofs that, after he attained his majority and was freed from the guardianship that kept him in Jerez, Cabeza de Vaca was appointed to a court post as chamberlain in the household of Medina Sidonia. Paradoxically, during his years in this post Cabeza de Vaca would serve the powerful Guzmán family, who had been bitter enemies of his famous grandfather Pedro de Vera. This information, though sufficiently reliable, tells us very little about Cabeza de Vaca's early youth. It is this recurrent scarcity of information capable of illuminating his person to which Enrique de Vedia was referring in the eighteenth century, in the prologue to his edition of the *Naufragios*, when he says that "details of his childhood and youth have not come down to us."[4]

Gradually, in more recent times, some bits of information have been revealed that fill in the outlines of Núñez's fragmentary biography. The Argentine historian Enrique de Gandía gathered a number of data that cast considerable light on Núñez's activities prior to his American experiences. Most of these are details and testimony obtained by de Gandía through a very careful reading of the evidence and documents gathered to defend Núñez from accusations that were made against him on his return from South America. But many of the deductions offered by de Gandía are speculative. However, other information that he contributes casts light on Cabeza de Vaca's military activities in Italy and Spain.[5] Though the information stated up to this point is based on reliable documentary sources, it does not tell us how long Cabeza de Vaca lived in Italy. What we can state is that he was back in Spain by 1521, when as an officer in the royal armies he took part in battles against Comunero groups. In particular, these documents refer to rebellions led by Juan de Figueroa in Seville that, as is well known, culminated in the capture of the Alcázar.

In alluding to these events and to himself, Cabeza de Vaca adds that he "found himself with the other knights and servants of the duke of Medina Sidonia in its [the Alcázar's] loss and recapture, in which he did great service to His Majesty, and thus Andalusia was secured."[6] We also know that the duke of Medina Sidonia, in addition to entrusting to Núñez the guarding of one of Seville's city gates, sent him with messages to the royal court, which was then in Valladolid. But, as often happens with minor figures during those centuries, between 1522 and 1523 we lose track of Cabeza de Vaca. He does not reappear in public life until 1527, when he joined the ill-fated expedition of Pánfilo de Narváez, the story of which forms the text of the *Naufragios*. Almost everything that was to happen to Cabeza de Vaca after his return to Spain is recorded in his own texts, in addition to the documents explicated by de Gandía and other historians. However, a recent study by the Spanish historian Juan Gil, of the University of Seville, has brought to light information about Núñez unknown until now. On Tuesday, 28 April 1506, Cabeza de Vaca appeared before the lawyer Rodrigo Guillén to make a number of claims, "and said that he is between the ages of eighteen and twenty-five years." This declaration places his date of birth closer to 1488 than to 1492. Professor Gil's investigations also corroborate the fact that relatives of Núñez's, like Fernando Ruiz Cabeza de Vaca, had access to influential circles in Sevillian society. Further, this study first identifies María de Marmolejo as Núñez's wife. The Marmolejos were prominent members of the Sevillian bourgeoisie and in their turn were related both to churchmen and to Jews.[7]

APPENDIX B

The American Cultures Described in Cabeza de Vaca's *Naufragios*

Native communities are described in the order assigned to them in Cabeza de Vaca's text.[1] All the tribes and clans described here lived in different stages of the Paleoindian period.[2] The chapters that relate to these tribes or clans are indicated when each culture is described.

CALUSAS

They were located in the parts of Florida to the south of Tampa, around Lake Okeechobee, and the present-day Everglades National Park. They also lived in the coastal areas of western Florida and were probably the first Indians encountered by Narváez's expedition. Nothing is known of their language, but it probably belonged to the Muskogee group. They had a social organization similar to that of the Timucuas and, like them, were exceptionally skilled in hunting and fishing. They generally lived in small communities and were believed to number three thousand persons. Early accounts by explorers refer to a ferocity that was probably defensive. As a tribe, the Calusas disappeared toward the end of the eighteenth century (chs. III–IV).

TIMUCUAS

They were located in the northern and central parts of Florida, chiefly in the area bounded today by Tampa, Orlando, and Ocala. Their name seems to be connected with the Withlacoochee (Tomoka) River, on whose banks they lived in a large number of villages. The basis of their language was believed to be Muskogee. In general they lived in small sedentary communities and raised riverbank crops, chiefly maize. They also hunted and fished. Their social organization had a hierarchical basis, partly defined by religious beliefs. Early in the eighteenth century the Timucuas began to mingle with other tribes; the disappearance of these separate cultures was accelerated by the advance of colonization (ch. V).

APALACHEES

According to Swanton, in the Muskogee language the word "apalachee" meant "people from the other bank" (Swanton, *Indians of Southeastern U.S.*, 216). Their language belonged to the Muskogee group and was likely similar to the variants spoken by the Hitchita and Alabama tribes. They lived in the extreme north of Florida and southern Georgia. Their chief population center was concentrated between Tallahassee and Apalachicola, the region in which Narváez's expedition encountered them. They formed sedentary communities grouped around the cultivation of maize (ibid., 89–93). Like the Calusas and Timucuas, they were skilled hunters and lived in physical and cultural proximity to the Creeks. Like the tribes previously described, the Apalachees lived in villages, preferably on the banks of rivers (Newcomb, *North American Indians*, 37). Narváez's expedition spent a good part of its first winter in areas occupied by Apalachees. The account by Cabeza de Vaca and those by De Soto's expedition all refer to the Apalachees' ferocity; but it must be stressed that the reactions of these Indians occurred after the invasion and attacks carried out by Spanish troops, as well as by other later groups of European colonizers. Like other neighboring tribes, they were adept in rituals related to warlike activity. The Apalachees too lost their distinct identity in the nineteenth century, mingling chiefly with Seminole groups (chs. VI–X).[3]

PENSACOLAS

These were coastal tribes who lived in the extreme northwest of Florida, specifically in the areas now occupied by the city that bears their name. They were also scattered throughout the approximate area between Pensacola and Mobile Bay, which the Indians pronounced "Mabila." They were very close to the Mobile and Choctaw tribes in their customs and degree of cultural development (Swanton, *Indians of Southeastern U.S.*, 150). In addition to fishing and hunting they cultivated maize, some vegetables such as beans and squash, and also tobacco; they possessed domesticated dogs. They achieved a type of pottery with clearly defined and distinctive designs (Newcomb, *North American Indians*, 42). Their language belonged to the Choctaw group, though with some Muskogee traits (ibid., 172). It is very probable that Narváez's expedition encountered them in the peninsulas and canals around the beautiful island of Santa Rosa (chs. VIII–XI).

KARANKAWAS

These tribes located on the coast and islands of eastern Texas had a seminomadic life, chiefly engaged in fishing, and settled as far south as the present-day city of Corpus Christi. The Karankawa communities consisted of little clans with many cultural similarities; among them were the Capoques, Coaques, Cocos, and Hans. These last, for example, belonged linguistically to the Atakapan family and concentrated in the vicinity of Galveston. The Indians Cabeza de Vaca describes on the Isle of Ill Fortune (Galveston Island) were Karankawas. The Copanes or Cobanes were located in areas close to the Brazos River. The first account of them that we possess is Cabeza de Vaca's. All those who describe them refer to the Karankawas' corpulence and the elaborate tattoos they displayed. Their homes were portable and were called *ba-ak* (Newcomb, *Indians of Texas*, 67–69). Like other neighboring tribes, the Karankawas practiced infanticide in special circumstances; they may have engaged in cannibalism, but this possibility is undocumented. They had elementary forms of pottery. Their linguistic base was believed to be mostly of Coahuiltecan, or more specifically of Uto-Aztekan, origin. Cabeza de Vaca lived for nearly a year with Karankawa clans (chs. XI–XVI).

CADDOES

Their culture was located in northwestern Texas and southwestern Arkansas and organized into widespread and complex confederations (Swanton, *Indians of Southeastern U.S.*, 98). These groups had cultural traits similar to those of the Meso-American cultures (Newcomb, *North American Indians*, 46–50) and also to the Nachitoche communities who lived in eastern Louisiana. The Caddoes were notable for the development and variety of their agriculture, and for the complex ritualization of their religious customs. Their language was sufficiently different from others to be labeled simply "Caddo." Hernando de Soto's expedition was the first to identify them. Cabeza de Vaca may have had contact with this culture when he was trading in areas near those that the Caddoes occupied. Some traces of their culture persist today in very small areas of the state of Oklahoma (ch. XVI).

ATAKAPANS

Little is known about these tribes who were called Akokisa by Spanish explorers. Some French explorers described Atakapans as cannibals (Swanton, *Indians of Southeastern U.S.*, 85). These groups were located in the extreme eastern part of Texas and western Louisiana. Their cultural development was very similar to that of the Karankawas. They may have been the ones Cabeza de Vaca calls "Han." Cabeza de Vaca perhaps had contact with them in the rounds that he made as a trader along those coasts (chs. XVI–XVII).

COAHUILTECANS

This culture, in its different variants, is the one that Cabeza de Vaca and his companions came to know best. Unfortunately for the Spaniards, the culture of the Coahuiltecans belongs to the most primitive stages of the Paleoindian period that modern archeology defines as "archaic." Nomadic clans of Coahuiltecans lived on the coasts of Texas, from the Brazos River to the Mexican border, but ranged as far inland as what is now the capital of Texas, Austin, in search of the cactus fruit and nuts that abounded near the basins and tributaries of the San Antonio and Colorado Rivers. These cyclical harvests and communal hunts for insects, reptiles, and occasional larger animals were their only means of subsistence; they knew little of agriculture and pottery. They carried their huts, which were very light, on their backs and used simple hunting implements; whenever circumstances permitted, they prepared some of their meals in holes in the rocks. Despite the rigors of the climate, they went naked. Their social organization seems to have been patriarchal. From Cabeza de Vaca's account we know that the Coahuiltecans used mesquite and prepared hallucinogens with peyote. Their language, though little known and little studied, is also called Coahuiltecan, though it belongs to the broad Meso-American group called Jocaltecan, which in its turn has numerous dialects (*Handbook,* 120). The group disappeared toward the end of the eighteenth century (Newcomb, *North American Indians,* 132–40). Cabeza de Vaca is speaking of them when he refers to Deaguanes, Mendicas, Mareames, Yguazes, Atayos, Acubadaos, Quitoles, Camoles, Queuenes, and Maliacones, among others (chs. XIX–XXVI).

JUMANOS AND CONCHOS

They lived in areas chiefly delimited by the Rio Grande and Concho River. Their language belonged to the broad Uto-Aztekan family, in its Taracahitan variant (*Handbook,* 121, linguistic map). Jumanos and Conchos were among the seminomadic groups who lived on the edges of those cultures that today are simply called "Pueblo." These communities in the northern part of present-day New Mexico and Arizona developed a distinctive style in weaving and pottery. The permanent communities had houses made of adobe, and the inhabitants cultivated maize and some vegetables. Eventually, like the Coahuiltecans, they mingled with other tribes who by the eighteenth century established themselves around the Spanish missions. Probably these groups were the ones whom Cabeza de Vaca calls Cattle People, for both the Jumanos and Conchos periodically hunted buffalo. Near them, and in the southern part of the area now occupied by the state of Arizona, were the Papagos; their culture was very close to that of the Jumanos in its customs and linguistic affiliation. The Papagos were sedentary and farmed in the valley of the Yaqui River. It is safe to assume that Cabeza de Vaca addresses them when he asks about the abundant source of maize (Newcomb, *Indians of Texas*, 225–45) (chs. XXIX–XXXI).

PIMAS

They lived in the northern area of the present-day Mexican state of Sonora and adjacent areas of the state of Arizona. According to the regions where they settled, they are usually referred to as High Pimas (near the Gulf of California) and Low Pimas. They shared with the Papagos and Opatas a linguistic connection of Uto-Aztekan origin. Culturally they were linked to the Papagos, and like them were efficient farmers who inhabited riverside communities in the valleys of the Gila River (Newcomb, *North American Indians*, 147). Like some of their neighbors, they had houses made of adobe and lived on extensive farmlands (chs. XXXI–XXXIV).

OPATAS

They lived in the central and eastern parts of Sonora and may have numbered twenty thousand persons. Their language had a Uto-Aztekan root, but the variant they used (Tahuina) has probably disappeared (*Handbook*, 320). They were independent tribes of farmers whose frequent wars with the Apaches and other cultures eventually united them (Newcomb, *North American Indians*, 129). Their communities began to disappear in the seventeenth century. Very probably the groups who followed Cabeza de Vaca and his companions, as well as the communities (in the "Village of the Hearts") described in the latter chapters of the *Naufragios* (chs. XXXII–XXXVI), were Pimas and Opatas.

Notes

INTRODUCTION

1. Some details of the landing are contained in the study by A. H. Phinney, "Narváez and De Soto: Their Landing Places and the Town of Espíritu Santo," *Florida Historical Quarterly* 3 (1925): 15–21. No definite landing place has been located.

2. Morris Bishop, *The Odyssey of Cabeza de Vaca* (1933; Westport, Conn.: Greenwood Press, 1971), 161. Núñez and his companions reached the capital of New Spain on 23 July 1536. It is not clear why they delayed so long in traveling from Culiacán to the viceregal capital. The historian Henry H. Wagner suggested—though without conclusive documentation—that Dorantes returned to Spain ("Alvar Núñez Cabeza de Vaca: *Relación*," in *The Spanish Southwest* [Berkeley: J. J. Gillick, 1924], 13).

3. Bishop, *Odyssey*, 169.

4. Ibid., 169–70. In these pages Bishop documents the known action of de Soto in asking Núñez to go with him.

5. I quote from Manuel Serrano y Sanz's edition of the *Relación* (*Colección de libros y documentos referentes a la historia de América* [Madrid: Librería General de Victoriano Suárez, 1906], 5:148).

6. Ibid., 23:8–23.

7. Bishop, *Odyssey*, 189.

8. It is estimated that Núñez invested about 14,000 ducats in the expedition. He left behind a debt of 5,000 ducats, a large sum in view of his assets (Serrano y Sanz, ed., *Colección*, 2:112, 147).

9. See Ulrico Schmidel, *Derrotero y viaje al Río de la Plata y Paraguay*, ed. R. Quevedo (Asunción: Biblioteca Paraguaya, 1983), 99–116; see also the report of Ruy Díaz de Guzmán, *Anales del descubrimiento, población y conquista del Río de la Plata*, ed. E. de Gandía (Buenos Aires: Librería Huemul, 1974).

10. On 7 December 1545 Cabeza de Vaca presented to the Council of the Indies the documents with which he intended to demolish the accusations of Irala and others; those documents place more emphasis on the calamities he suffered than on factual refutation.

11. Bishop, *Odyssey*, 279.

12. Enrique de Gandía, "Aventuras desconocidas de Alvar Núñez

en Italia y en España," in *De la Torre de Oro a las Indias* (Buenos Aires: Ediciones L. J. Rosso, 1931), 121. Gonzalo Fernández de Oviedo also tells us that "they took him as a prisoner to the court, where, weary and poverty-stricken, he continues his suits against his rivals, and it is very pitiful to hear him and learn what he suffered in the Indies" (Fernández de Oviedo y Valdés, *Historia general y natural de las Indias,* ed. Juan Pérez de Tudela [Madrid: B.A.E., 1959], 2:190, 371). The same complaints about calamitous experiences are echoed by Núñez's scribe, Pedro Hernández, who says in his *Comentarios,* "And after having held him prisoner and confined to the court for eight years, they released him and he departed; and because of some suits that were brought against him they stripped him of his governorship . . . without having recompensed him for the large sums of money that he spent in the service he performed, of going to aid and discover" (*Comentarios* [Madrid: Taurus, 1969], ch. 84).

13. Fernández de Oviedo, *Historia general,* 2:271. Thomas Buckingham Smith reproduced—in translation—documents, petitions, and allegations taken from the Archive of the Indies, as well as from other sources that deal with Núñez's unsuccessful appearances before the Council of the Indies (*Relation of Alvar Núñez Cabeza de Vaca* [New York: J. Munsell, 1871], 231–35.

14. Buckingham Smith, *Relation,* 231–33. See also a royal warrant of 8 April 1573 located by de Gandía, which authorized Pedro Hernández "to return to New Spain . . . and to take a mestizo son of his, without giving information" (de Gandía, "Aventuras," 124).

15. De Gandía, "Aventuras," 123. His study reproduces documents that shed light on the circumstances in which Cabeza de Vaca died.

16. Our present knowledge of the seventeenth-century book market in Spain does not allow us to describe the success attained by Cabeza de Vaca's *Relación* as "enormous" (as Roberto Ferrando does in his recent edition of the *Naufragios* [Madrid: Historia 16, 1984], 14). Printed books about America had an average audience that included a small minority of educated people and those officials interested in very specific aspects of the texts in question; however, over the course of centuries Núñez's narrative achieved considerable international circulation. On the making and marketing of books in the sixteenth century see Konrad Haebler, *The Early Printers of Spain and Portugal* (London: Chiswick Press, 1896–1897); and on the printing of books in the sixteenth and seventeenth centuries see Clive Griffin, *The Crombergers of Seville: The History of a Printing and Merchant Dynasty* (Oxford: Oxford University Press, 1988). See also Antonello Gerbi, *La naturaleza de las Indias Nuevas* (Mexico City: Fondo de Cultura, 1975), 265–306; 445–64. The large amount of documentation on New World historiography that Gerbi amassed focuses on the work of Fernández de Oviedo.

CASTAWAYS

1. Charles V (1500–1558). In my critical edition of the Spanish text, *Los Naufragios* (Madrid: Editorial Castalia, 1992), I offer an approximate chronology of Cabeza de Vaca's route and identify other historical personages as well as geographical references and those relating to flora, fauna, measurements, and distances.

2. Different versions of this narrative give the seventeenth and the twenty-seventh. The dates used by Cabeza de Vaca refer to the Julian calendar. Ten days must be added to adapt them to our modern calendar.

3. We can only estimate the equivalent of the sixteenth- and seventeenth-century league; it is thought to be just under three miles. In this narrative references to geography tend to be vague. The port called Cabo de Santa Cruz (ch. I) is the Bay of Santa Cruz, on the western coast of Camagüey province, Cuba. The name Bay of Horses (ch. IX) was made up on the spot by the Narváez contingent.

4. Narváez's expedition had a very faulty knowledge of the regions around the Gulf of Mexico. The river of Las Palmas is thought to be in Tamaulipas, Mexico, and is known today as Soto la Marina. However, Cleve Hallenbeck (*Alvar Núñez Cabeza de Vaca* [Port Washington, N.Y.: Kennikat Press, 1971], 23) suggests that the river of Las Palmas is the Rio Grande, which runs along the border of the United States and Mexico.

5. It is located on the extreme western tip of Cuba.

6. This is apparently Tampa Bay, in an area near Boca Ciega.

7. The reference is to the southernmost part of Georgia and northern and northwestern Florida.

8. Pánuco was in fact about 900 miles west of Tampa.

9. It is unlikely that the Spaniards could understand the complex gestures and sign language used by the natives.

10. Apalachee is probably a village near present-day Tallahassee, Florida.

11. Núñez refers to a town in Andalusia, in Spain.

12. This is an Indian community in the basin of the Apalachicola River, not far from Tallahassee.

13. A *fanega* is a measure roughly equivalent to one bushel.

14. This is the narrow entry portion of Apalachee Bay, Florida.

15. The party had reached the Mississippi.

16. This is Galveston Island.

17. The "little dog" was possibly a raccoon (*Procyon lotor*).

18. Graphic illustrations and narratives in the sixteenth and seventeenth centuries frequently describe the natives as being extremely tall.

19. The roots probably came from the plant known as the swamp potato (*Sagittaria L.*).

20. The distance of two crossbow shots is about one hundred yards.

21. Cabeza de Vaca's calculation is incorrect: ninety-six soldiers had survived.

22. The reference is to a parasitic plant known as Spanish moss (*Tillandsia usneodes*).

23. Almost all the tribes and clans identified by Cabeza de Vaca belonged to the Coahuiltecan culture that was distributed along the coasts of the Gulf of Mexico.

24. Some scholars have suggested, erroneously, that Cabeza de Vaca reached the region now occupied by the state of Oklahoma.

25. After this period the chronology of Cabeza de Vaca's narrative becomes increasingly uncertain.

26. This "arm of the sea" is Matagorda Bay, Texas.

27. The nuts come from the pecan tree (*Cayra olivaeformis*).

28. The fruit is from a cactus (*Opuntia vulgaris*) found in many parts of Texas.

29. In analyzing the construction of this text, we must keep in mind that parts of Cabeza de Vaca's narrative reflect oral statements given him by others, in differing versions.

30. The enigmatic and evocative reference to Esquivel's book suggests that the report transmitted to Cabeza de Vaca by Esquivel, through Figueroa, may have a textual basis—possibly the only written source for Cabeza de Vaca's narrative.

31. The events recounted here must have taken place about the summer of 1529, and thus we infer that these survivors were with the Yguazes and other neighboring tribes for almost four years. So prolonged a stay presupposes periods of intimate association, made inevitable by the need to survive. The culture of these tribes and clans is associated with the early American Paleoindian (see Appendix B and ch. XXI).

32. It is believed that this beverage was prepared with peyote (*Lophophora williamsii*), a plant with narcotic properties.

33. Mistakenly, Cabeza de Vaca seems to interpret all ceremonial rites as festive occasions. Using the Taino word, he describes them indiscriminately as *areitos*.

34. This is the first European report of the existence of the American buffalo (*Bubalus bubalis*).

35. The approximate time lapse was from January 1532 to July 1533. For the chronological details offered by Cabeza de Vaca, see my critical edition (hereafter CE).

36. This tribe or clan lived in the coastal areas of southeastern Texas. Almost all these tribes, which Cabeza de Vaca encountered as

groups of hunters and gatherers who spoke similar dialects, disappeared early in the nineteenth century.

37. Such references indicate that Cabeza de Vaca and his companions learned to use and distinguish six or seven of the dialects spoken in areas fairly close to present-day San Antonio, Texas, and neighboring regions of northern Mexico.

38. Some students of Cabeza de Vaca's itinerary believe that he was then in the valley of the Llano River. See CE and the studies of Hallenbeck and Krieger listed in the bibliography.

39. Ever since the sixteenth century, this description has caused major controversies among students of Cabeza de Vaca's journey. Leading historians such as Francisco López de Gómara (1512–1572) characterized Cabeza de Vaca as a person who claimed to possess supernatural powers.

40. With this chapter, Cabeza de Vaca's authority as narrator and leader becomes more pronounced.

41. Cabeza de Vaca's description of this figure resembles other representations of the Devil by many chroniclers of the Indies. See CE and Sabino Sola, *El diablo y lo diabólico en las letras americanas* (1550–1770) (Bilbao: Publicaciones de la Universidad de Deusto, 1973).

42. The narrator seems to refer to the "shoal waters" of Texas, the time of year when water freezes in rivers and shallow creeks (see the prologue to Buckingham Smith, *Relation*).

43. These events must have occurred about August 1535.

44. Very possibly these were domesticated coyotes (*Canis latrans*).

45. Before 1527 Cabeza de Vaca had taken part in military campaigns in Italy.

46. On the anthropological significance of this passage see CE.

47. A more detailed identification of these tribes and clans appears in Appendix B. Cabeza de Vaca uses various spellings when he refers to bands of Coahuiltec Indians (for example, Cutalches and Cutalchiches in ch. XXII). These casual phonetic transcriptions become less fixed in his mind with the passing of time. For the sake of consistency in this edition I have chosen the spellings used most frequently.

48. Peyote when burned could produce smoke. But a number of researchers, among them William W. Newcomb, suggest that the material used could have been tobacco mixed with other ingredients. Tobacco was cultivated in many areas adjacent to the Gulf of Mexico (*North American Indians* [Pacific Palisades, Calif.: Goodyear Publishing, 1974], 40).

49. An *arroba* equals twenty-five pounds.

50. Cabeza de Vaca's important observation establishes the fact that homosexuality was tolerated and describes ways in which it affected the distribution of labor.

51. The fruit of this plant (*Prosophis julixflora*) resembles a medium-

sized bean. The Indians ground it to make flour, which they mixed with water.

52. Cabeza de Vaca refers to the Guadalquivir.

53. The phrase is ambiguous and applies to either the Gulf of Mexico or the Pacific Ocean.

54. It was probably not silver but rather the mother-of-pearl portion of shells.

55. Cabeza de Vaca and his companions appear to have been in communities of Opata Indians, who lived in areas adjacent to the Bavispe River basin in the state of Sonora, Mexico.

56. This is sulphate of lead, a silvery white metallic chemical element that was used in the sixteenth century in medicines and pigments.

57. The narrator refers to the Pacific Ocean.

58. Anticipating modern anthropological practice, Cabeza de Vaca describes the cultural development of Indian communities by listing the foodstuffs with which they were familiar.

59. This is the stone called chalchuite or *chalcheuitl* by the Navajos. It is found encrusted in the striations of rocks and owes its sky-blue color to the heavy concentration of copper it contains.

60. This settlement would be close to the present-day town of Ures, some 45 miles from the Pacific Ocean and about 15 miles to the south of Hermosillo (Cleve Hallenbeck, *Alvar Núñez Cabeza de Vaca* [Port Washington, N.Y.: Kennikat Press, 1971], 230).

61. *Bohío* is the Taino word for a hut. Cabeza de Vaca often applies words of Taino origin, which he had learned in Cuba, to objects and rites that he encountered in the southwestern United States and northern Mexico.

62. This village must have been near San José de Delicias, in the mountains of northwestern Sinaloa (Hallenbeck, *Alvar Núñez*, 239).

63. Diego de Guzmán reached the Yaqui River in Mexico.

64. This meeting took place somewhere between Sinaloa and Ocoroni (Hallenbeck, *Alvar Núñez*, 240). Friar Antonio Tello described the incident: "Cabeza de Vaca, Estebanico, and eleven Indians met Captain Lázaro de Cárdenas and three mounted men at Los Ojuelos, a day's journey from Tzinaba, on the Petatlán River" (*Libro segundo de la crónica miscelánea en que se trata de la conquista espiritual y temporal de la santa provincia de Jalisco en el Nuevo Reino de la Nueva Galicia y Nueva Vizcaya y descubrimiento del Nuevo México* [Guadalajara: Imprenta de la República Lituana, 1891], 186).

65. San Miguel was a community near the city of Culiacán, which was founded in 1531.

66. According to Buckingham Smith, Cabeza de Vaca incorrectly transcribed this word from the Opata tongue (*Relation*, 189).

67. Cabeza de Vaca and his companions arrived in Culiacán on

1 April 1536. It is worth noting that the Crown's chroniclers and historians scarcely allude to the conflict that arose between Cabeza de Vaca and the Spanish military.

68. The Marqués del Valle was Hernán Cortés (1485–1547); the meeting took place on 25 July 1536.

69. This incident has a decidedly imaginative ring to it, and the sentence quoted in Portuguese is grammatically incorrect; see CE.

70. This sentence in the third person suggests the participation of a scribe in preparing the first edition of 1542.

71. Hornachos is a town in the province of Badajoz that was well known in the sixteenth century for having a large population of Moriscos and converted Jews.

72. The Moroccan town of Azamor or Acemur is located at the mouth of the Um-Er-Rebia River. On the identity of this personage and the legends that grew up about him, see John Upton Terrel, *Estevanico the Black* (Los Angeles: Westernlore Press, 1968).

73. Correct Latin would be *Deo gratias* (Thanks be to God).

APPENDIX A

1. See Manuel Serrano y Sanz, ed., *Colección de libros y documentos referentes a la historia de América*, vol. 6, (Madrid: Librería General de Victoriano Suárez, 1906).

2. See Hipólito Sancho de Sopranis, "Notas y documentos sobre Alvar Núñez Cabeza de Vaca," *Revista de Indias* 91–92 (1967): 207–44; and the following articles by de Sopranis: "Datos para el estudio de Alvar Núñez Cabeza de Vaca," *Revista de Indias* 27 (1947): 69–102; "Pedro de Vera hasta su gobierno de Gran Canaria," *Revista de historia* 1 (1955): 17–28. Other valuable information is summarized in Morris Bishop, *The Odyssey of Cabeza de Vaca* (1933; Westport, Conn.: Greenwood Press, 1971).

3. De Sopranis proves the existence of a number of persons named Alvar Núñez Cabeza de Vaca who, to compound confusion, were also residents of Jerez ("Notas," 221).

4. Enrique de Vedia, ed., *Historiadores primitivos de Indias* (Madrid: Biblioteca de Autores Españoles, 1946), 21:517.

5. In particular de Gandía clarifies, and for the first time, the sequence of historical events in which Núñez was involved. See Enrique de Gandía, "Aventuras desconocidas de Alvar Núñez en Italia y en España," in *De la Torre de Oro a las Indias* (Buenos Aires: Ediciones L. J. Rosso, 1935) 101–4.

6. Ibid., 111. See also Enrique de Gandía, *Historia de la conquista del Río de la Plata y del Paraguay* (Buenos Aires: Ediciones L. J. Rosso, 1931).

7. The study by Juan Gil will be published shortly in *Anuario de estudios americanos: Sección de historiografía y bibliografía americanista.*

APPENDIX B

1. The descriptions of the communities encountered by Núñez are based on information from the following texts: *Handbook of North American Indians*, vol. 10, ed. Alfonso Ortiz (Washington, D.C.: Smithsonian Institution, 1983); William W. Newcomb, Jr., *North American Indians: An Anthropological Perspective* (Pacific Palisades, Calif.: Goodyear Publishing, 1974); and, by the same author, *The Indians of Texas* (Austin: University of Texas Press, 1962); John R. Swanton, *The Indians of the Southeastern United States* (New York: Greenwood Press, 1969). I have also consulted the following studies: Lyle Campbell and Marianne Mithun, *The Languages of Native America: Historical and Comparative Assessment* (Austin: University of Texas Press, 1979); Jean D. Umiker-Sebeok and Thomas E. Sebeok, *Aboriginal Sign Language of the Americas and Australia*, vol. 2 (New York: Plenum Press, 1972).

2. Life in the Paleoindian period was organized around cyclical emigrations connected with hunting or with gathering fruits, nuts, or roots with nutritional value. These nomadic modes of subsistence were supplemented by consumption of other plants, insects, and small animals. The technology of these cultures was characterized by the use of stone, bones, snails, and fibers obtained from many different plants. Almost all the cultures that Núñez described, and especially the Jumanos, Caddoes, and Opatas, belonged to the terminal phases of this period.

3. In a number of previous editions of the *Naufragios*, the Seminoles are incorrectly described as among the aboriginal cultures encountered by Narváez's expedition. Groups of Indians known by this name from other fragmented cultures in Florida joined together to form new communities early in the eighteenth century. The Seminoles probably accepted Negro slaves who had escaped from the plantations (Newcomb, *North American Indians*, 39).

Select Bibliography

EDITIONS OF THE *RELACIÓN* OR *NAUFRAGIOS*

Núñez Cabeza de Vaca, Alvar. *La relación que dio Alvar núñez cabeça de Vaca de lo acaescido en las Indias en la armada donde yua por gouernador Pamphilo de narbaez desde el año de veynte y siete hasta el año de treynta y seis que boluio a Seuilla con tres de su compañia.* Zamora, 1542.

———. *La relacion y comentarios del gouernador Alvar núñez cabeça de vaca de lo acaescido en las dos jornadas que hizo a las Indias.* Valladolid, 1555.

———. *Navfragios de Alvar Núñez Cabeza de Vaca, y Relación de La jornada que hizo a la Florida con el adelantado Pánfilo de Narváez.* In *Historiadores primitivos de las Indias Occidentales, que junto, traduxo en parte y sacó a la luz, ilustrados con eruditas notas y copiosos índices, el ilustríssimo Señor D. Andrés González Barcia,* vol. 1. Edited by Andrés González Barcia Carballido y Zúñiga. Madrid, 1749.

———. *Naufragios de Alvar Núñez Cabeza de Vaca y relación de la jornada que hizo a la Florida con el adelantado Pánfilo de Narváez.* Edited by Enrique de Vedia. Biblioteca de Autores Españoles, vol. 22. Madrid: Imprenta y Estereotipía de M. Rivadeneyra, 1852.

———. *Relación de los naufragios y comentarios de Alvar Núñez Cabeza de Vaca.* Vol. 5 of *Colección de libros y documentos referentes a la historia de América.* Edited by Manuel Serrano y Sanz. Madrid: Librería General de Victoriano Suárez, 1906.

Fernández de Oviedo y Valdés, Gonzalo. *Historia general y natural de las Indias.* Vol. 4, 285–318. Edited by Juan Pérez de Tudela. Madrid: B.A.E., 1959.

———. *Naufragios y comentarios.* Edited by Roberto Ferrando. Madrid: Historia 16, 1984.

———. *Naufragios.* Edited by Trinidad Barrera. Madrid: Alianza Editorial, 1985.

———. *La relación o naufragios de Alvar Núñez Cabeza de Vaca.* Edited by Martín E. Favata and José B. Fernández. Potomac, Md.: Scripta Humanistica, 1986.

———. *Naufragios.* Edited by Enrique Pupo-Walker. Madrid: Editorial Castalia, 1992.

Hart, Billy Thurman. "A Critical Edition with a Study of Style of *La Relación* by Alvar Núñez Cabeza de Vaca." Ph.D. diss., University of Southern California, 1974.

TRANSLATIONS OF THE *RELACIÓN*
OR *NAUFRAGIOS*

Núñez Cabeza de Vaca, Alvar. *Relatione che fece Alvaro Nvnez detto Capo di Vacca: Di quello che interuenne nell'Inde all'armata, della qual era gouernatore Pamphilo Naruaez, dell'anno 1527 fino al 1536.* Vol. 3 of *Delle navigationi et viaggi.* Translated by Giovanni Battista Ramusio. Venice: Nella Stamperia d'Givnt, 1565.
————. *Relation et naufrages d'Alvar Núñez Cabeça de Vaca.* Vol. 7 of *Voyages, relations et mémoires originaux pour servir à l'histoire de la découverte de l'Amérique.* Translated by Henri Ternaux-Compans. Paris: Arthur Bertrand, 1837.
————. *Relation of Alvar Núñez Cabeza de Vaca.* Translated by Thomas Buckingham Smith. 1851. New York: J. Munsell, 1871.
————. *The Journey of Alvar Núñez Cabeza de Vaca.* Translated by Fanny Bandelier. 1905. New York: A. S. Barnes, 1973.
————. *Schiffbruche Die Unglücksfahrt der Narváez-expedition nach der Südküste Nordamericas in den jahren 1528 bis 1536.* Translated by Franz Termer. Stuttgart: Strecker und Schroeder, 1925.
————. *Cabeza de Vaca's Adventures in the Unknown Interior of America.* Translated by Cyclone Covey. New York: Collier Books, 1961.

STUDIES ON CABEZA DE VACA
AND HIS WRITINGS

Books

Belloguín García, Andrés. *Vida y hazañas de Alvar Núñez Cabeza de Vaca.* Madrid: Editorial Voluntad, 1928. Partial version.
Bishop, Morris. *The Odyssey of Cabeza de Vaca.* 1933. Westport, Conn.: Greenwood Press, 1971. The best, though fictional, biography of Cabeza de Vaca.
————. *Cabeza de Vaca's Great Journey.* Washington, D.C.: Pan American Union, 1942.
Fernández, José B. "Contributions of Alvar Núñez Cabeza de Vaca to History and Literature in the Southern United States." Ph.D. diss., Florida State University, Tallahassee, 1973.
————. *Alvar Núñez Cabeza de Vaca: The Forgotten Chronicler.* Miami: Ediciones Universal, 1975. Descriptive study that summarizes interesting research.
Hallenbeck, Cleve. *Alvar Núñez Cabeza de Vaca: The Journey and Route*

of the First Europeans to Cross the Continent of North America, 1534–1536. Port Washington, N.Y.: Kennikat Press, 1971.

Long, Haniel. *The Power Within Us: Cabeza de Vaca's Relation of His Journey from Florida to the Pacific, 1528–1536.* New York: Duell, Sloan, and Pearce, 1944. A free translation of Núñez's text.

———. *The Marvelous Adventure of Cabeza de Vaca and Malinche.* Prologue by Henry Miller. London: Pan Books. 1983. Partial and somewhat breathless account of the facts. (First published as *La merveilleuse aventure de Cabeza de Vaca suivie de Malinche [Doña Marina].* Paris: Hollier, 1970.)

Rodman, Maia. *Odyssey of Courage: The Story of Alvar Núñez Cabeza de Vaca.* New York: Atheneum, 1965. Partial version.

Swanton, John R. *The Indians of the Southeastern United States.* New York: Greenwood Press, 1969. Though originally published at the turn of the century, this work is still a standard reference.

Urdapilleta, Antonio. *Andanzas y desventuras de Alvar Núñez Cabeza de Vaca.* Madrid: Instituto de Cultura Hispánica, 1949. Partial version.

Shorter Studies

Barrera López, Trinidad. "Problemas textuales en los *Naufragios* de Alvar Núñez Cabeza de Vaca." *Historiografía y bibliografía americanistas* 30, no. 2 (1986): 21–30.

Baskett, James Newton. "Study of the Route of Cabeza de Vaca." *Quarterly of the Texas State Historical Association* 10 (1907): 246–79, 308–40.

Bost, David H. "The *Naufragios* of Alvar Núñez Cabeza de Vaca: A Case of Historical Romance." *South Eastern Latinoamericanist* 27 (1983): 3–12.

Chipman, Donald E. "In Search of Cabeza de Vaca's Route Across Texas: An Historiographical Survey." *The Southwestern Historical Quarterly* 91 (1987): 127–48.

Coopwood, Bethel. "The Route of Cabeza de Vaca." *Quarterly of the Texas State Historical Association* 8 (1899): 108–40; 3 (1900): 229–64; 5 (1900): 1–32; 7 (1900): 177–208.

Davenport, Herbert. "The Expedition of Pánfilo de Narváez by Gonzalo Fernández de Oviedo." *The Southwestern Historical Quarterly* 27 (1923): 120–39; 28 (1924): 124–63.

Davenport, Herbert, and Joseph K. Wells. "The First Europeans in Texas, 1528–1536." *The Southwestern Historical Quarterly* 22, no. 2 (1918): 111–42; 22, no. 3 (1919): 205–59.

Dowling, Lee. "Story versus Discourse in the Chronicle of the Indies: Alvar Núñez Cabeza de Vaca's *Relación.*" *Hispanic Journal* 5, no. 2 (1984): 89–99.

Gandía, Enrique de. "Aventuras desconocidas de Alvar Núñez en

Italia y en España." In *De la Torre de Oro a las Indias*, 101–4. Buenos Aires: Ediciones L. J. Rosso, 1935.

Gómez Aguirre, Carlos E. "Introducción al estudio de la crónica de Alvar Núñez Cabeza de Vaca." *Repertorio americano* 4, no. 2 (1978): 18–25.

Griego y Bravío, Alicia. "Alvar Núñez Cabeza de Vaca: Un jerezano en lo desconocido." *Cádiz/Iberoamérica* 2 (1984): 41–43.

Krieger, Alex D. "The Travels of Alvar Núñez Cabeza de Vaca in Texas and in Mexico, 1534–1536." In *Homenaje a Pablo Martínez del Río: Los orígenes americanos*, 459–75. Mexico City: Instituto Nacional de Antropología, 1961.

Lafaye, Jacques. "Los milagros de Alvar Núñez Cabeza de Vaca (1527–1536)." In *Mesías, cruzadas, utopías: El judeo-cristianismo en las sociedades ibéricas*, 65–84. Mexico City: Fondo de Cultura, 1984. (First published as "Les miracles d'Alvar Núñez Cabeza de Vaca, 1527–1536." *Bulletin hispanique* 64 [1962]: 136–53.)

Lagmanovich, David. "Los *Naufragios* de Alvar Núñez como construcción narrativa." *Kentucky Romance Quarterly* 25 (1978): 22–37. Analysis of the text's fictional dimension.

Lastra, Pedro. "Espacios de Alvar Núñez: Las transformaciones de una escritura." *Cuadernos americanos* 204, no. 3 (1984): 150–63. (Also published in *Revista chilena de literatura* [1984]: 89–102.)

Lewis, Robert E. "Los *Naufragios* de Alvar Núñez: historia y ficción." *Revista iberoamericana* 48, nos. 120–21 (1982): 681–94.

Molloy, Sylvia. "Formulación y lugar del 'yo' en los *Naufragios* de Alvar Núñez Cabeza de Vaca." *Actas del Séptimo Congreso de la Asociación Internacional de Hispanistas* 2 (1980): 761–66.

Pastor, Beatriz. "Desmitificación y crítica en la relación de los Naufragios." In *Discurso narrativo de la conquista de América*, 294–337. Havana: Casa de las Américas, 1983.

Pupo-Walker, E. "Los *Naufragios* de A. Núñez Cabeza de Vaca: Notas sobre la relevancia antropológica del texto." *Revista de Indias* 47, no. 181 (1987): 755–76.

———. "Notas para la caracterización de un texto seminal: Los *Naufragios* de A. Núñez Cabeza de Vaca." *Nueva Revista de Filología Hispánica* 38, no. 1 (1990): 163–96.

———. "Los *Naufragios* de Alvar Núñez Cabeza de Vaca y la narrativa hispano-americana." *Quinto centenario* (Universidad Complutense de Madrid) 6, no. 2 (1988): 38–56.

Sopranis, Hipólito Sancho de. "Datos para el estudio de Alvar Núñez Cabeza de Vaca." *Revista de Indias* 27 (1947): 69–102.

———. "Notas y documentos sobre Alvar Núñez Cabeza de Vaca." *Revista de Indias* 23 (1961): 207–41.

Wagner, Henry R. "Alvar Núñez Cabeza de Vaca: Relación." *The Spanish Southwest, 1542–1794*. Berkeley: J. J. Gillick, 1924.

Index

Compositor: Impressions, a division of Edwards Brothers
Text: 10/12 Palatino
Display: Palatino
Printer and Binder: Edwards Brothers